THE IDEAL LOVE-RELATIONSHIP

Discover the science to create your ideal lasting love-relationship

Shantiom Mumtaz Mahal

Foreword by Barbara Raji

Copyright ©2015 Shantiom Mumtaz Mahal. All Rights Reserved.

Published by Hasmark Publishing

1-888-402-0027

No part of this book may be reproduced or transmitted in any form or by any means, electronic or mechanical, including photocopying, recording or by any information storage and retrieval system, without written permission from the author, except for the inclusion of brief quotations in a review.

Disclaimer: This book is designed to provide information and motivation to our readers. It is sold with the understanding that the publisher is not engaged to render any type of psychological, legal, or any other kind of professional advice. The content of each article is the sole expression and opinion of its author, and not necessarily that of the publisher. No warranties or guarantees are expressed or implied by the publisher's choice to include any of the content in this volume. Neither the publisher nor the individual author(s) shall be liable for any physical, psychological, emotional, financial, or commercial damages, including, but not limited to, special, incidental, consequential or other damages. Our views and rights are the same: You are responsible for your own choices, actions, and results.

Permission should be addressed in writing to: shantiom@theideallove-relationship.com

Editors, Barbara Raji & Roger Savage

Cover Design, Patti Knowles

Layout Assistant (Shantiom's fingers), DocUmeant Designs
www.DocUmeantDesigns.Com

First Edition, 2015

ISBN-13: 978-1-988071-09-1
ISBN-10: 1988071097H

WHAT READERS ARE SAYING ABOUT THE IDEAL LOVE RELATIONSHIP

"The Ideal Love-Relationship is unique, philosophical and fascinating. If you would love to understand why you are the way you are, and create your ideal love relationship, read Shantiom's book now."

—**Peggy McColl, New York Times Best-Selling Author**

"After many difficult lessons in this world Shantiom Mumtaz Mahal will soon be ready to live in her magic Love-Relationship with her beloved Soul-Mate and Best Friend."

—**Barbara Raji**

"In the book Shantiom Mumtaz Mahal shows you step by step through her seven magical steps.... how to live your ideal Love-Relationship......"

—**Bob Proctor**

This book is dedicated to my beautiful and beloved SOUL-MATE, my Soul's other half, whom I LOVE with my whole heart and who has been my best friend, my wonderful husband and lover, best business partner, best co-worker in leading countries, most loving, romantic, sexy companion in countless lifetimes. Who also woke me up in this life and gave me hope about experiencing my IDEAL LOVE-RELATIONSHIP even in this life and beyond.

I believe in LOVE and LOVE is the strongest force as well as the essence of our SOUL.

CONTENTS

SPECIAL THANK YOU xi

FOREWORD xv

INTRODUCTION xvii
    Why 'The Ideal Love-Relationship'? xvii
    The Ideal Love-Relationship and The
        Seven Magic Goal Steps To Success! xxii

CHAPTER 1: HAVING HAD INHARMONIOUS LOVE-RELATIONSHIPS IN THIS LIFE I DISCOVERED A PAST HARMONIOUS IDEAL LOVE-RELATIONSHIP FROM A PREVIOUS LIFE! 1

CHAPTER 2: BASIC RELATIONSHIP FOUNDATION–TO FIND OUT WHERE WE ARE TODAY! 23
    The Influenced Baby 29
    The Mixed Baby 30
    The Aware Baby 31
    The Seven Levels of Awareness 32
    My Babyhood 34

CHAPTER 3: HEALING OF THE HEART 37
    The exercises of the heart will help us heal our heart and move out of our false comfort zone into our true comfort zone where we can rest comfortably and use it as a base before we create our ideal love-relationship 37
    Things That I Didn't Like About My Childhood . . . 39

Forgiveness About My Childhood 40

Things That I Liked About My Childhood 41

My Ideal Childhood 42

Things That I Didn't Like About My Youth 43

Forgiveness About My Youth 44

Things That I Liked About My Youth 45

My Ideal Youth 46

Things That I Didn't Like About My Past
    Love-Relationship(s) 47

Forgiveness About My Past
    Love-Relationship(s) 48

Things That I Liked About My Past
    Love-Relationship(s) 49

Things That I Don't Like About My Present
    Love-Relationship 50

Forgiveness About My Present
    Love-Relationship 51

Things That I Like About My Present
    Love-Relationship 52

CHAPTER 4: THE IDEAL LOVE-RELATIONSHIP AS OUR GOAL IN A GREATER PERSPECTIVE 55

    THE SOUL = The Science Of Universal Living . . . 55

    The Universal Process on Earth 57

    The Healthy Natural Human Process In Life 59

    The Seven Levels of Awareness 60

    The Seven Levels of Awareness Described from the
        Bottom Upwards: 61

CHAPTER 5: THE IDEAL LOVE-RELATIONSHIP AND THE SEVEN MAGIC GOAL STEPS TO SUCCESS-SEEKING MORE OF ALL KINDS! 65

    The Seven Levels of Living 66

    My Soul-Master's Message about the
    Seven Levels Of Living.. 67

    The Golden Rule Of Success = ...71

    Let Us Have a Look at the Formula for the
    Seven Goal Steps To Success!. 73

    How We Live in the Body with
    The Seven Levels of Living 78

    The Seven Magic Goal Steps To Success
    — The Whole Process 80

    No 7, The Goal, My Ideal Love-Relationship. 84

    We Create 7, THE GOAL with 1, NEW IDEA AND 2, CREATE. 85

CHAPTER 6: THE IDEAL LOVE-RELATIONSHIP AND THE SEVEN MAGIC GOAL STEPS TO SUCCESS! 0, WHERE WE ARE AND 3, THINKING 91

    ... and We Have Special Focus on Building Our Self-Image and Our Common Self-Image. 91

CHAPTER 7: THE IDEAL LOVE-RELATIONSHIP AND THE SEVEN MAGIC GOAL STEPS TO SUCCESS! 4, IN LOVE. 101

    1. The Instant Infatuation (Passion) 101

CHAPTER 8 FEAR => COMMUNICATION => KNOWLEDGE THE SEVEN MAGIC GOAL STEPS TO SUCCESS, 5. GRATITUDE AND FORGIVENESS 107
    2. The Developing Infatuation (Passion) 107

CHAPTER 9: SOUL-MATES AND KARMA-MATES . . . 113
    Persistence and Perseverance = Loving Patience Towards Ourselves and Others. 113
    Soul-Mates lost in worldly games 114
    Coming together with Soul-Mates and how you can uplift each other. 116
    Spiritual Love-Life vs. Worldly Love-Life 118
    Different Roles in Different Lifetimes as Humans (Homosexuality). 121

CHAPTER 10: LOVE, SEX AND ROMANCE AND OTHER EMOTIONS 125
    - Learn To Recognize Your Emotions 125
    - Gratitude Opens Up for The Highest Faculty of the Mind–Compassion 125
    - The Ideal Love-Relationship and The Seven Magic Goal Steps To Success! 125
    2, The Developing Infatuation (Passion) 125
    Compassionate, Emotional Forgiveness. 130
    Grateful for Emotions Both Positive, Peaceful and Negative 131

CHAPTER 11: YOU GET TO YOUR RESULTS BY MOVING WITH ACTIONS OF LOVE AND A JOYFUL, PLAYFUL ATTITUDE 137
   The ideal love-relationship and the seven magic goal steps to success! 6 Actions 137
   3. The Playful Infatuation (Passion) 137

CHAPTER 12: WHAT IS A LIVING MIND-MASTER AND A PERFECT LIVING SOUL-MASTER. 143

CHAPTER 13: YOUR DREAMS COME TRUE!!! 147
   The Ideal Love-Relationship and The Seven Magic Goal Steps To Success! 7, The Goal, The New Freedom 147
   - 3, The Playful Infatuation (Passion). 147

CHAPTER 14: SUMMARY OF 'THE SEVEN MAGIC GOAL STEPS TO SUCCESS' 153
   Constantly Improving the Ideal Love-Relationship to Keep It Successful 153
   What Is Your Vision? 154
   MY VISION—Love Castle—Love Couples 154

SHANTIOM MUMTAZ MAHAL. 157

SPECIAL THANK YOU

THANK YOU SOUL-MASTER for your grace and blessings and for always being with me and supporting me with your Love and Compassion with the highest awareness possible through the audible life stream.

THANK YOU SOUL-MATE For your LOVE, compassion and passion, for being my IDEAL LOVE-MATE, the other half of my own Soul.

THANK YOU MIND-MASTER BOB PROCTOR for your wise thinking and great knowledge about life and the universal laws and for your enlightening and encouraging words. You are a living example of SUCCESS.

THANK YOU Dr. RANDOLPH STONE D.C, D.O., Polarity teacher and therapist for so lovingly having taught me Polarity Therapy, the law of Polarity and other valuable things about life.

THANK YOU BENNO GRALSBORG for being such a good Polarity teacher, Esoteric teacher, iridology therapist, homeopath, Esotherapist with your big heart and compassion.

THANK YOU BARBARA RAJI for your loving help and suggestions and for editing and proof reading the book. And thank you for your encouragement so that I never gave up my dream of creating my book about The ideal Love-Relationship.

THANK YOU ROGER SAVAGE for editing my book to perfection, and for your fast and efficient work. It was a pleasure working with you. Thank you for your advice and encouragement.

THANK YOU PEGGY McColl for your expertise knowledge and willingness to share it in The Millionaire Author Intensive class and The Total Author Immersion seminar in Sarasota, Florida. You are a living example of a SUCCESSFUL AUTHOR.

THANK YOU JUDY O'BEIRN for your expertise and intense work with the book that makes it possible for me to become a BEST SELLING AUTHOR. You have both persistence and belief.

THANK YOU PATTI KNOLES for your magic creativity and persistence in creating a beautiful book cover and symbol that took me closer to my dream of realizing my first book.

THANK YOU COLIN MILLER who made my website possible with beautiful and creative designs. You have a clean fresh radiance through your webpages.

THANK YOU TRACE HASKINS for your professional creativity, fantasy and you are an expert of playing with words and creating me a great sales page.

THANK YOU THE CREATIVE TEAM APPLE STORE EMPORIA, MALMO, SWEDEN, thanks to you this book was possible to create. You have shown me possibilities beyond my knowledge.

THANK YOU TO MY PARENTS for your invaluable economic support so that I could realize my dream of becoming an international successful author and Ideal Love-Relationship teacher.

THANK YOU TO MY CHILDREN: My daughter Caroline 20 years old, my son Daniel 18 years old and my son Ted 14 years old for your loving support and patience and that you always believed in me and that I could have International success despite it was a long waiting for all of us.

THANK YOU AND MUCH LOVE TO YOU

Shantiom Mumtaz Mahal

FOREWORD

After many difficult lessons in this world Shantiom Mumtaz Mahal will soon be ready to live in her magic Love-Relationship with her beloved Soul-Mate and Best Friend.

All the time she has been guided by her perfect living Soul-Master both on the inside and on the outside and people have when necessary been sent into her life to ease her struggle and accompany her on her way in life. Now she wants for the first time to share her experiences with you and help you to find your perfect Love-Relationship. Many books will follow this one when she and her Soul-Mate together will be a powerful Love-Package that has a lot to offer to the world.

Barbara Raji

INTRODUCTION

WHY 'THE IDEAL LOVE-RELATIONSHIP'?

I really wanted to know what it's all about and what is the ultimate LOVE and the ultimate ideal Love-relationship with your Soul-Mate.

I have been studying my mentor and teacher, THE MIND-MASTER Bob Proctor's teachings for ten years now and my absolute favorite program of his is: "The Success Puzzle".

It tells you so much about how things work in the world and the definition of SUCCESS which his mentor and teacher Earl Nightingale passed over to him.

Here is his quote:

> "Success is the progressive
> realization of a worthy ideal."
>
> Earl Nightingale

I quote Bob Proctor about this piece of wisdom from his teacher and mentor Earl Nightingale:

"That is the best definition of SUCCESS I have ever found. His definition is in perfect harmony with the laws of the universe."

Bob Proctor

Bob Proctor encourages us to think of how important each of the four words: <u>progressive, realization, worthy and ideal</u> are in this quote.

What does each of these words mean to you?

PROGRESSIVE: _____

_____

_____

REALIZATION: _____

_____

_____

WORTHY: _____

_____

_____

IDEAL: _____

_____

_____

"I found out that when I can prioritize and combine my own spiritual development coupled with my ideal LOVE-Relationship I am the happiest person I can possibly be."

Shantiom Mumtaz Mahal

I have tried to combine the best of my Soul-Master's teachings and the Mind-Master Bob Proctor's teachings as well as I could in this book. I have included the study of myself as a child and of my parents, as we need to know where we are and the experience we have with us before we move forward to our ideal Love-Relationship; and I have found out that there are three major types of children and they have parents and an environment that are more or less developed than they are.

With this understanding about ourselves before we study how we can create our Ideal Love-Relationship we are very well equipped to deal with our own paradigm (multitude of habits) before we have to deal with somebody else's paradigm that has nothing to do with our old habits of thinking, feeling and behaviour.

When we want to live our ideal Love-Relationship we want to be free from our old paradigm (multitude of habits) and negative behaviour as much as possible because we don't want our old paradigm to stop us from being happy with our loving spouse in our ideal Love-Relationship. We have to have a kind of cleansing period within ourselves before we create and go into our ideal Love-Relationship and identify ourselves and where we are.

We may be very impatient to create and to get to our ideal Love-Relationship, but if we are moving too fast without knowing where we are we may get into unnecessary problems.

I am also describing a couple of my past lives where I begin to understand the magic (law) of cause and effect, and it's three actions.

There are three categories of babies: THE INFLUENCED BABY, THE MIXED BABY AND THE AWARE BABY and we learn to identify ourself as a baby, which helps us understand more about ourself.

Before we create our ideal Love-Relationship we have to know where we are as a basic relationship foundation which I call 'The healing of the Heart' and 'The exercises of the Heart', where we go through a lot of our past experiences. We go from a 'false comfort zone' to a more 'genuine authentic comfort zone' and rest harmoniously there before we start to create our Ideal Love-Relationship. The four exercises of the heart move from 'I didn't like', to 'I forgive', to 'I am grateful', to 'My ideal'. We study 'THE SOUL'='The Science Of Universal Living' in a greater perspective, so that we can widen our perspective.

Then throughout the whole book we study: THE IDEAL LOVE-RELATIONSHIP AND THE SEVEN MAGIC GOAL STEPS TO SUCCESS. 'The magic (law) of perpetual increase' is the highest level with humans at the top of the pyramid in 'The seven levels of awareness.'

We can be differently developed in different areas of our life in 'THE SEVEN LEVELS OF LIVING'.

What is 'THE GOLDEN RULE OF SUCCESS'?... That which all serious Successful people know about.

We work for our own future in 'THE MAGIC (LAW) OF CAUSE AND EFFECT':

1. Actions (karmas) in the now

> Here we create certain things in the now and for the future. We do our best and use wisely 'The highest faculties of our mind' and create our own destiny.
>
> Remember compassion is the highest faculty of the mind. We act as if this is the only life that we have!

2. Stored actions (karmas)

> When we have had actions in past lives and we have not yet received the results/the effects because they are stored for us for our future for a better time for us to give or receive.

3. Stored destined actions (karmas)

> Depending on our past lives and our past behaviours, there is a certain destiny in this life that we have to go through. We can either do it willingly or unwillingly and we can either do it smilingly or tearfully and sometimes we do both...

THE IDEAL LOVE-RELATIONSHIP AND THE SEVEN MAGIC GOAL STEPS TO SUCCESS!

We are going from 0 The Comfort Zone, to no 1 'The New Idea', and to 2 'Create', then to 0 'The Comfort Zone'-where we are and then we go to 3 'Thinking', where we build up our SELF-IMAGE.

Knowing where we are, from your memory to your new thoughts, think yourself out of your old paradigm (multitude of habits).

Think from the comfort zone and create a new paradigm. Where I am no matter if I am alone or in an existing Love-Relationship.

Ask yourself if you are in an existing Love-Relationship:

> **Do I want to stay in this Love-Relationship?**
>
> **Are we in agreement about working together towards a common ideal Love-Relationship?**

Enjoy identifying yourself and your surroundings both from the past and the present.

In 4, 'IN LOVE' is about 'The Instant Infatuation' (passion), we study with our 'Higher Faculty of The Mind' PERCEPTION and observe where we are and how we vibrate in the body together with our emotions.

And the three necessary ways of falling IN LOVE for a **successful Love-Relationship.**

1. The instant infatuation (passion)
2. The developing infatuation (passion)
3. The playful infatuation (passion)

In 5, 'GRATITUDE AND FORGIVENESS' we study:

To overcome fear necessitates good communication. Communication is the basic foundation for a successful relationship.

FEAR => COMMUNICATION => KNOWLEDGE

To overcome fear necessitates good communication. Communication is the basic foundation for a successful relationship.

'The developing infatuation' (passion)

PERSISTENCE AND PERSEVERANCE = THE LOVING PATIENCE TOWARDS OURSELVES AND OTHERS, and we can be 'in loving disagreements' with our loved one.

Soul-mates and Karma-Mates (karma=exchanges of giving and receiving) and the difference. Sharing your life with your Soul-Mate can be the ultimate Ideal Love-Relationship especially in the end of our stay (lifetimes) here on earth.

THE IDEAL LOVE-RELATIONSHIP AND THE SEVEN GOAL STEPS TO SUCCESS! 5, GRATITUDE AND FORGIVENESS

To overcome the seven negative emotions and replace them with the seven neutral emotions and the seven positive emotions filled with compassion and love for ourselves and others.

- -LOVE, SEX AND ROMANCE AND OTHER EMOTIONS
  - -LEARN TO RECOGNIZE YOUR EMOTIONS
  - -GRATITUDE OPENS UP FOR THE HIGHEST FACULTY OF THE MIND – COMPASSION

THE IDEAL LOVE-RELATIONSHIP AND THE SEVEN GOAL STEPS TO SUCCESS! 6 ACTIONS.

Use your will power and strength to move with actions into your new Love-Relationship.

3, 'The Playful Infatuation' (passion)

YOU GET TO YOUR RESULTS BY MOVING WITH ACTIONS OF LOVE AND A JOYFUL, PLAYFUL ATTITUDE.

WE ALSO STUDY WHAT A LIVING MIND-MASTER **AND** A PERFECT LIVING SOUL-MASTER ARE.

FINALLY!

THE IDEAL LOVE-RELATIONSHIP AND THE SEVEN GOAL STEPS TO SUCCESS! 7, THE GOAL, THE NEW FREEDOM, The ultimate LOVE-Freedom I love YOU unconditionally!

I accept and love you the way you are.

And then enjoy creating and living your ideal Love-Relationship with a higher awareness of yourself.

CONSTANTLY IMPROVE THE IDEAL LOVE-RELATIONSHIP TO KEEP IT SUCCESSFUL!!!

Shantiom Mumtaz Mahal

"THE TRUE DIVIDING LINES FOR MANKIND ARE NOT BORDERS, COLOR OR LANGUAGE, BUT SIMPLY <u>IGNORANCE</u> AND IT'S POLAR OPPOSITE, <u>UNDERSTANDING</u>."

BOB PROCTOR

 # CHAPTER 1

HAVING HAD INHARMONIOUS LOVE-RELATIONSHIPS IN THIS LIFE I DISCOVERED A PAST HARMONIOUS IDEAL LOVE-RELATIONSHIP FROM A PREVIOUS LIFE!

I was born into a family where the Love-Relationship between my parents was very undeveloped.

Some of my earliest memories go back to when I was about 2-3 years old and I heard my parents argue and fight with each other with unkind words again and again. It always ended with my mother crying and my father being very angry. I was the only child, and when I was unhappy because of their arguing and needed comfort, I always went to my collie dog Sussie because she was the only one I could turn to for comfort. I always cried when they were arguing and fighting and I always ended up crying with my head on my dogs tummy. My parents didn't notice me at all, as they were so busy with their own feelings and hurts and forgot all about me and how I felt: they were only thinking of themselves.

When I was exposed to this scenario with my parents I remember how I always thought: "I wish I could help them to become more happy with each other."

I have written this book based on experiences from my own life and studies and that has helped me to understand myself more so that I can live better and share my ideal Love-Relationship with my spouse.

Having studied my parents closely when I was a child, I can now easily explain where they were in 'The seven levels of awareness' pyramid.

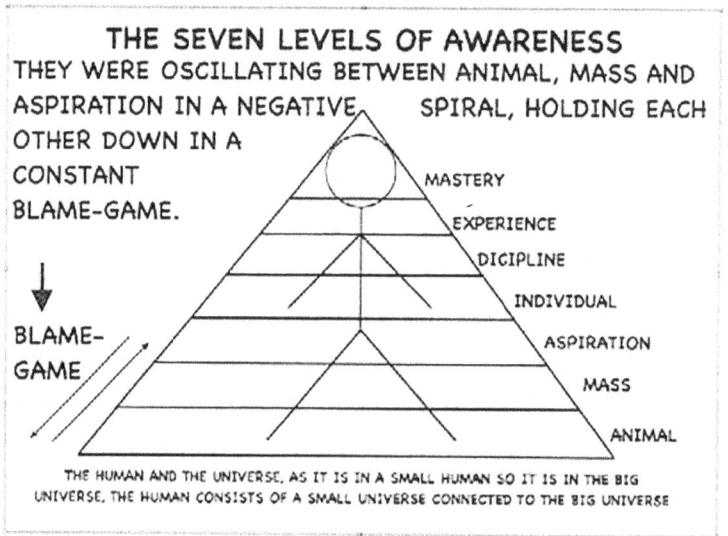

My Parents' Blame-Game

My parents were desperately blaming each other back and forth between the animal-mass-aspiration states, and if one of them wanted to aspire to an individual state the other was there to press them down in different ways.

My mother was crying and depressed and turned inwards and my father was angry and upset and turned outwards, and I was their unhappy witness watching them play a yoyo game all the time where they were loving and happy together one day and the next day they were behaving terribly towards each other.

Chapter 1

Later on I became their 'marriage counselor' when they took turns approaching me about the problems they had with each other.

I listened and said a few words here and there, but I realized very soon that they were so busy thinking about themselves and that they were really not interested enough in each other and didn't have enough communication, compassion and forgiveness for each other in order to improve their relationship.

They were arguing about money, greediness, jealousy, how the lawn was supposed to be cut, what to watch on TV, how I should be treated, if we should have more pets, just anything! All the time my mother demanded that my father should help her with the household chores because my father demanded that she should help him with all kinds of chores in the stores, so it always ended with a great disagreement.

The most happy times my parents had were when they decided to create something together and especially after they bought their first store when I was eight years old. When they agreed in their planning of their stores and worked towards the same goal they were happy, but my father was very clumsy and complained about my mother in front of others, which of course made her mad and unhappy. They were both jealous which resulted in that they hardly had any friends. This is an example of two people who are at that level of awareness in their Love-Relationship where they actually are harming each other without realizing what they are doing because of their selfish motives which they believe is the only way to behave.

My First Boyfriend

This is what happened to me:

My dad wanted me to marry a man who worked in one of his stores so that we could take over the stores after him.

But when I was 16 years old I met a two year older man who was from America and my dad became terrified that I should move to America.

All the years before I met him, my dad had been speaking well about America, but after I had met this man my dad started to talk badly about America in order to try to make me afraid of moving there as he didn't want to lose me; but he failed to terrify me.

As I had taken over the paradigm (multitude of habits) of not communicating well with others from my parents, it was one of the reasons why the relationship with my first boyfriend ended and there were also so many other things in our lives that we didn't have in common, so the karma (the exchange of give and receive) was finished.

Much later I found out that this first boyfriend had, in his past life, been my maternal grandfather.

When I was a young girl I had a chat with God, as my mother had been so fond of her father, my grandfather, and he died three years before I was born and two weeks after my parents' wedding and my mother never stopped mourning him. I have now learned that you cannot demand anything from God or anybody, you must either pray or ask for it, but I put a demand on God, and said:

Chapter 1

"I want to meet my grandfather that I have heard my mother talk so much about before I am 12 years old or else I won't believe in you."

I even meant his spirit, but as I did not meet him it resulted in me becoming an atheist at the age of 12.

My mother was already an atheist. (Maybe because she found it so hard to loose her dad, whom she was so fond of, that she lost her faith in God.) An atheist is someone who doesn't believe in God or anything.

So without knowing it I met my own grandfather at the age of 16 and fell in love with him in his new body and he was only two years older than me, so he was reborn a year after he died.

God answered my prayer at his own time and in his own way. My boyfriend who in his previous life had been my grandfather, was now reborn but this time in America and he had a Swedish mother and an American father in this life. When his parents were divorced he came back with his mother to live in Sweden and we met at a seminar. Whenever he came and visited me in our house he was always welcome, for both my mother and my grandmother liked him very much without knowing who he had been in his past life, and I didn't know either during the almost 10 years we were together that he was my previous grandfather. But he taught me the difference between an atheist and an agnostic and I found out that I was not an atheist I was an agnostic. An atheist doesn't believe in God or anything, but an agnostic believes in something, though doesn't know exactly what.

(Today I believe in the power of God and have realized that I am being guided back to my own soul and origin by my spiritual Soul-Master.)

When I met my boyfriend I was 16 years old and had been a lacto vegetarian since I was 8 years old and I didn't want to kiss him when he had been eating meat, fowl or fish. He really had to change, a lot in order to be together with me and at home we only had vegetarian meals too. I also had to change, and that was my alcohol intake, and my drinking habits became worse. (Today I know I degraded myself spiritually by drinking alcohol.) I was not used to alcohol at all and he wanted to drink both beer and wine with me and I was too weak to say no although I didn't like to drink it. I did it both for his sake and social reasons with him and our friends.

My alcohol consumption was changed and stopped drastically when I was poisoned at a bar drinking only one glass of beer which made me so sick for a whole day. A few months later the relationship ended.

He didn't want to be a vegetarian and I didn't want to drink alcohol and we had learned how different we were with our wants in life and we had grown apart from each other and the karma (the exchange of give and receive) was finished.

Chapter 1

The Father of My Three Children

My former boyfriend was practicing karate when he lived in America and continued to do so when he moved to Sweden. But after a few years' break he wanted to practice it again and he also took me to a karate class.

My boyfriend wanted very much to meet the head of the his Karate School in Sweden whom he had heard so much about and of course it was my future husband that became our teacher. He was the best karate performer in Sweden with the highest degree of black belt and had graduated from the Japanese Karate School and was the founder of the Swedish section. He travelled to clubs all over Sweden and also the world, both as an instructor and as an international judge.

A few months before the relationship with my boyfriend ended I fell in love with our karate teacher. I wanted to be honest and finish the relationship I had with my boyfriend before I started the new relationship with my karate teacher.

Our karate teacher told me later that he didn't want to approach me because I was together with my boyfriend. So, when my boyfriend and I decided, in a very friendly way, to end our Love-Relationship and he moved out of my apartment, I told my karate teacher, after I had struggled with my mind for months, that I was in love with him and he immediately said that he also was in love with me. From that day we were a couple.

Everything happened within three months. So first: from the day my boyfriend and I broke up and he moved out—the second—it took three months before my karate teacher and I were a new couple. The third: three months later I became pregnant with our first baby. This was a typical western way of starting a new Love-Relationship by letting 'The magic (law) of attraction' be the leading magic (law) which brought us fast into the new relationship in a physical binding way.

When we started to reason with each other, we mostly had very opposite opinions: I wanted to get married and he didn't want to get married, I wanted to live in the countryside and he wanted to live in the city, I wanted us to start out in a new house together and he didn't want to move out of his own house, I wanted to do things with him and he didn't want to change his old lifestyle, I was more playful and he more serious and reserved, I wanted to travel with him, but he didn't want to take me on his trips except for once a year, I wanted his company daily, but he didn't want to be together with me except for a late evening meal after he had finished his work, I wanted to discuss how we should live our life together, but he wanted me to handle it by myself so he could continue to live the separate life he always had lived, I wanted our children to have their own rooms, but he didn't, and he also didn't want to be too much together with the children or take care of them either, it was my job he thought, I wanted kindness and love, but he treated me in a degrading way with mean and harsh words which often made me cry.

Chapter 1

My clumsy movements mirrored how his bad behaviour and criticism made me feel. I now realise that the only way our relationship survived for so long was because I gave and gave and gave.

And still I gave everything good I could to him because I believed that LOVE could solve everything. What I was not aware of was that when we give the best we can in a relationship where we have to stay due to karma (the exchange of give and receive) we actually create good karma for future relationships.

When I went somewhere I mostly brought my children with me, but since my husband didn't want to share his life with me most of the time, most people who met me thought I was a single mom.

I wanted to make a paradise garden for my children and although I had a tiny garden with poor soil I created a lovely garden and planted many beautiful flowers, vegetables and berries. I was working very hard to make the garden look as beautiful as possible. I used the work in the garden as a very good therapy to get rid of unwanted thoughts and to surround myself with beauty. Then I bought some nice playhouses, slides, swings, swimming pools, tents and a lot of other things for the children. It was a small garden but I made it as cozy as I possibly could.

I also arranged parties, mostly Halloween parties, for the children where they could invite everybody in their classes and they were a great success, but my husband didn't want to participate as usual and when I wanted to invite friends to the house he didn't want to participate either, often staying in his office.

In Sweden many families celebrate birthdays by bringing a breakfast tray and gifts to the birthday child who stays in bed. Everybody stands around the bed singing the birthday song holding their gifts, flowers and birthday cards in their hands. Then everybody watches the birthday child while he or she opens the gifts.

My husband never liked to participate in these celebrations and often refused to leave his bed.

When the children had problems in their school and needed to change school I had the usual resistance from my husband who didn't want to get involved at all. He always preferred things to remain the same, he hated changes.

But when the children had made the change to their new school, he appreciated it very much, after having scolded me for a long time before the change finally took place. The change of school was a great blessing and success and really helped the children in their development as youngsters by giving them self-confidence and good education and they also developed their musical abilities as they played various instruments and gave performances on several occasions. My husband didn't want to marry me, but I managed to talk my husband into marrying me because I wanted to be initiated by a perfect living Soul-Master and start to meditate and live according to his instructions. One of the rules is that you have to be married to the person you have sex with and I was very persistent about wanting to receive initiation and start my inner spiritual journey by meditating daily. And within a few days after I had asked my husband to marry me we were all of a sudden married.

Chapter 1

We only had a small wedding and only our two children were attending the wedding.

My parents and my husband's older children were too negative about us being together so we chose not to invite them.

It was not my ideal dream wedding, I wanted a fairytale wedding, but at least I got what I needed so that I could start my inner spiritual journey.

But as soon as I started to meditate my husband didn't like me spending so much time on my spiritual practice and made fun of me, but I continued my spiritual practice no matter what he said.

Then I used most of my time studying and when I started to study Bob Proctor's book 'You Were Born Rich' I began to clear the house of all excess things and then the flow of abundance began in the house. As I had learned from my childhood that I could find comfort with my dog, I started to buy all kinds of animals to replace the sadness I felt by being abandoned by my husband.

Both the children and I were interested in animals and we started to collect animals of many kinds. I overdid it because I was so unhappy in my marriage. We had fish, a parrot, almost 50 rabbits, 11 cats, 8 dogs and 10 horses and as we lived in a rather small house with a rather small garden we had to rent a place for the horses. My husband used to complain every day about the animals, although he accepted me buying them in the beginning, and asked me several times to move out of the house and when I finally did move out he didn't want me to do so and even denied that he had ever asked me to move out.

When I was hardly able to move forward and prayed to my Soul-Master for help he sent me an "angel".

And the new karma brought a lot of exchanges of give and receive.

My friend, who was at the age of a grandmother, immediately was adopted by my children as their grandmother when she came into the family. I had been crying a lot because of my situation, but after she came into the house I started gradually to change my attitude for the better. She both helped me to make order in the house and change the children's and my attitude for the better, and she even helped my youngest son to start to speak. I met my friend at meetings with my Soul-Master. She was not so popular with my parents and my aunt and cousins because they only wanted the family circle to remain as it always had been or else they became jealous. For me, the children and our dogs she was a blessing, and I had been praying to my Soul-Master for help right before she came into our lives, so that I would survive my situation.

My husband didn't like changes so when we were cleaning and clearing the house he would complain a lot. He wanted everything to remain as it "always" had been.

How I was grateful that she came to us. She was going to stay with us for a night and then go with us to a meeting with our Soul-Master, and then she saw my situation and took pity on me and wanted to help me.

Chapter 1

That was the beginning of a lifelong friendship and a new family member.

I also know that she has been a close family member both to me and the children in many incarnations.

My husband and I had a long relationship that lasted for 18 years and resulted in three beautiful children.

I couldn't practice the ideal Love-Relationship with him either because of the karma (exchange of give and receive) we had between us.

When I tried to communicate with him he withdrew and didn't want to talk with me because he thought I demanded too much. And then he started to speak in a mean way to me, but there still was enough attraction to have three children with him.

The children and I had a terrible and lonely time because I was missing having a husband and best friend and they were missing a father to do things with.

When we take 'The magic (law) of cause and effect' even called 'The magic (law) of karma' into consideration, we have to learn that most Love-Relationships go under that magic (law) and in a karmic relationship you mostly have to pay for what you have done or not done in a past life or past lives, but however you can always plan and work towards your ideal Love-Relationship!

Our Past Life In a Former Reincarnation Affected Us In Our Daily Life

By the very end of our relationship I had learned what our main karma (the exchange of give and receive) was and what we owed each other of give and receive.

Thousands of years ago in ancient Egypt both my father and I were the reigning Pharaoh and my ex-husband (in this life) was my wife. I was the natural successor to my father therefore he had taught me how to give advice to people and companies. We worked very hard and successfully together and our country flourished under our influence. My father was also my Soul-Mate and we had a very harmonious relationship.

Unfortunately my wife was very interested in the power we had and wanted to lead the country instead of us.

My father and I could read her thoughts telepathically and knew about her hunger for power that she would misuse in a negative way. We knew that she was not satisfied with "only" being a mother and a queen and taking care of all the servants at the palace, but wanted the power that we possessed.

As her husband I knew what she was up to so I avoided her, and both my father and I knew it would be a catastrophe for the country with her in the leading position so we never let her take part in the politics of the country. I worked mostly with my father and tried to avoid my power crazy, furious and demanding wife as much as possible. We even started to educate my eldest son a little earlier than

Chapter 1

normal so that we could educate him as much as possible.

This went on until that day when my wife had had enough of her wife-, mother-and queen-life and wanted the power that my father and I had and she had us both killed. Then she took over all our assets and the throne and she even had my two favorite lions killed.

Our eldest son ran away and hid himself and didn't come back until his mother had died and then he claimed the throne after her and then slowly and slowly he built up the country again from the chaotic state it had been in during the reign of his mother.

When I analyse that life with the help of 'The magic (law) of cause and effect,' 'The magic (law) of karma':

I can see the results from that life in the karma (the exchange of give and receive) that I had to go through with the father of my three children:

I was left alone with the children most of the time and he didn't care much for me. I had to pay for this because I had left my former wife in Egypt alone a lot, but my husband had to give me back my two favourite lions in the form of two collie dogs that I received as gifts on my 35th birthday. Then when I divorced him I claimed my legal half of the house which he owed me from what he had done to me in our past life in ancient Egypt when he was my wife and had me killed and took over all our assets.

My Parents' Fears

As my dad always had a lot of fears he often was dominant and he tried to force me and scare me instead of being kind and let me do things in my own way.

When my mother let fears take over she was often overprotective too. She tried with her fears to talk me into something by explaining why she thought I should do so, while my dad tried to force me into something by trying to make me afraid and suspicious of everything and everybody.

I tell you this, not because I want to be negative or say bad things about my parents, but to teach you who want to learn more about yourself and your ideal Love-Relationship what consequences a negative attitude can have both in a Love-Relationship and how you as a child can be formed by it.

Therefore I have come to the conclusion that we need a system that will make it easier for us to understand what we have experienced as children with our parents and guardians and in our past Love-Relationships so that we can understand where our paradigm (multitude of habits) is coming from and learn to easier let go of the old habits that we don't benefit from in our relationships and development today.

We should also be aware of 'The magic (law) of cause and effect' even called 'The magic (law) of karma', that can put us in situations where we are very much aware of what is happening, but we have to pay a price for our past actions from this and past lives.

When I was a child I could reason and think a lot, but I could not remember my past lives, which I started to do much later as an adult.

Chapter 1

I Have Already Been Living In My Ideal Love-Relationship

Then I found out that I had been living in my ideal Love-Relationship together with my Soul-Mate in Ireland in the first half of the 19th century.

Throughout my own history of lifetimes I can see myself striving towards my ideal Love-Relationship and finally I could experience it in the most beautiful way.

As I am a woman who loves comfort, I even in that life experienced my life in a big mansion almost like a castle with everything I could wish for including being together with my beloved Soul-Mate in a loving, beautiful, romantic way. I thought I was the happiest woman on earth and I was in a constant state of joy and happiness. I walked around with big a smile on my lips and my whole being vibrated and radiated with the powerful positive love, romance and creative sexy energies that were part of my life. I was married to the most kind, loving, sensitive, beautiful, handsome, caring, giggling, humorous, romantic, sexy, man I could imagine.

We were healthy and wealthy and we had the most beautiful, harmonious, loving, strong, romantic, powerful, sexy, giggling relationship I could imagine.

As my husband had a high position in society he was active in politics and took care of all the business and I was responsible for the household with all the servants and our six children. We were cultivating our own food and we had a beautiful domain with a beautiful garden. We lived a happy and playful life.

We also used to invite people to our beautiful mansion for parties.

My husband and I studied tantra with the esoteric approach and we were practicing tantra together. That was our greatest common interest. We meditated and used our bodies like laboratories and experimented with the energies. One thing we often practiced together was looking into each others eyes sharing the inner beauty with each other. Our common goal was to spiritually connect and raise our awareness and at the same time enjoy and share the raised progressive pleasure in our bodies while making love. The combination is a durable beautiful outstanding pleasure, like a long orgasmic feeling all over the body consciously connected with the emotions, mentally and spiritually.

When we connected like that, we forgot about ourselves and became one with each other all the way from the spiritual to the physical and the other way around.

Beautiful!

Wow, I was in a constant state of happiness and so was my husband.

We had a big bed in front of a fireplace in our bedroom, and we often made love in the evenings when the warmth from the fireplace made it comfortable. The palm leaves on the wallpaper in our bedroom also enhanced the beauty of the room. Both of us were totally in harmony with ourselves and each other.

I think it is the most happy, harmonious, healthy, wealthy, loving marriage I've ever had.

Chapter 1

Besides making love with my husband, study tantra and meditate, I loved to take care of our children and our home. My husband and I played a lot with our children and I tried to be the best mother possible and I know that my children loved me. (and that has been confirmed from one of them in this present life). Love vibrated all throughout our home in details and as a whole, in the material and in the non-material. Our life seemed perfect, but I still had a heavy lesson to learn: My husband passed away before me, and I became shocked and helpless. I realized how emotionally weak I was despite all the meditation and tantra training. I was very much attached to my husband. He was my whole world. Without him I lost myself emotionally and became depressed. I developed a desire to be able to communicate with him on the other side, but I never managed to do that in that life.

I brought the desire with me to my present life and, after I had met and fallen in love with my Soul-Mate in this life, the old shock and fear of loss became a paradigm for me, which I didn't understand at first and why I attracted a situation where I was more or less left to strengthen myself and to learn to love myself more and more and more. I have also learned to give myself material gifts as well as emotional, intellectual and spiritual gifts.

After I have met my Soul-Mate in this life my highest ideal Love-Relationship goal is to get reunited with him again in a happy loving ideal Love-Relationship in all levels of living and beyond into eternity. That has really kept me motivated and to grow in awareness as a result. As we both have had other karmas to pay with other people, I have been forced to see how 'The magic (law) of cause and effect' (give and receive) works and that you can't always have what you want immediately, but you can work towards it and develop yourself while waiting for the good that you desire and you can do it with a good positive attitude as the base that you always come back to knowing that at some point in time you will be reunited with your Soul-Mate.

Falling in love with my Soul-Mate again made me grow very much in awareness and that also motivated me to want to share with others how beautiful and loving an ideal Love-Relationship can be and the wonders of love, romance and the sexual creative power among a whole lot of other things in a relationship, which has resulted in this book that you are now reading!

"THE LAW OF ATTRACTION IS ALWAYS WORKING, WHETHER YOU BELIEVE IT OR UNDERSTAND IT OR NOT."

BOB PROCTOR

"EVERYONE HAS A COMFORT ZONE DETERMINED BY PREVIOUS CONDITIONING. THE IMPORTANT THING IS TO BE WILLING TO GROW AND TO CHANGE."

BOB PROCTOR

 # CHAPTER 2

BASIC RELATIONSHIP FOUNDATION – TO FIND OUT WHERE WE ARE TODAY!

Our comfort zone and what impressed and what impresses our life up to now, paradigms (multitude of habits) and karmas (exchanges of different experiences with different people).

We prefer to live in our present comfort zone where we are well used to our paradigm (multitude of habits) sometimes consciously and sometimes subconsciously. That is where we are before we get the desire to change our lives for the better. When we want to create our ideal Love-Relationship we first of all have to know where we are and we have to be 'comfortable' in our authentic comfort zone so that it isn't a false comfort zone (false picture of ourselves) that we live in.

We come with a package of good and bad experiences from the past and that has an effect on our relationships today, even if we haven't been aware of it before and worked with it consciously.

When we are born into this world we often adapt to other people's habits and way of thinking and if we are born with an open mind we absorb the better or the worse more easily and we also trust the parents and the closest people we have around us more.

If the parents do good things the babies might want to do good things and if the parents do bad things the babies might want to adapt to that, and if the babies watch TV, internet or other media they often copy what they say or do there too.

If we are born with an open mind and are positive, we can get a lot of advantages, but if we take in a lot of negative things we will have to overcome them when we want to develop ourselves in awareness.

And furthermore children who completely trust adults and their surroundings are able to resist absorbing automatically the habits and thoughts around them (both good and bad) and they are also able to reason a little more than those who are completely open.

These children have some areas in their lives that need to be developed a little more and other areas that already are well developed.

There are however some children that don't accept being formed by the bad paradigms of their parents and other close people and media and those children are more developed than their parents and their surroundings.

There are three major categories of babies that are interesting to study and when we have identified our category as babies we can start to examine our own parents if they were more or less developed than us and what we have learned from our experiences in our childhood.

Did we adapt to most of the things that our parents did or did we reason and select some of it or did we think and reason completely freely?

Actions

Actions also mean to take the trouble to study ourselves and create something new in our mind, but we should not undertake actions in the outside world before we are really ready for it.

Our development to a higher awareness and to something new in the world make us repeat the same patterns until we are ready to go to the new patterns with a higher awareness and new experiences in the world as a result. When people talk about actions in the self development industry they refer to actions both in the physical world, and as well as actions in our mind!

Similarly when we want to create our ideal Love-Relationship our first actions start in _our_ mind when we study ourselves and others around us and really try to get to know what _our_ ideal Love-Relationship is about.

PARADIGM – MULTITUDE OF HABITS

- THE FIRST THING WE NEED TO DISCOVER IS WHAT PARADIGM WE ADAPTED FROM OUR PARENTS, ASK YOURSELF: WHAT DID I ADAPT?

- THE NEXT THING IS: DID I ADAPT SOMETHING FROM SOMEBODY ELSE, PERHAPS THE MEDIA, OR SOMEWHERE ELSE? AND IF YES, WHAT WAS THAT?

- CREATE AND FILL IN THE HEART THAT WE HAVE IN THE END OF THE CHAPTER AND TAKE TIME TO RECOGNIZE YOUR PARADIGM AND WHERE IT COMES FROM.

- BUT FIRST YOU SHOULD READ THE FOLLOWING ABOUT THE DIFFERENT TYPES OF BABIES AND GET A CLEARER PICTURE OF YOURSELF AND YOUR PARENTS.

Chapter 2

Three categories of babies -
Which category did I belong to as a baby?

I have chosen to divide babies into three major categories to make it easier for us to find out how our development was as a baby.

And within these categories of babies we can try to examine whether our parents' behaviour were more or less aware than ours.

The babies within the three thought filters have a chance to develop themselves to a higher degree of thinking, understanding and awareness no matter where they are.

However some of them may have more resistance from themselves and others, but that can also result in very big changes and conscious shifts in their thinking for the better.

We are often very developed in some areas of our lives, but underdeveloped in other areas and in some areas we also have more karma (exchanges of give and receive) to pay through 'The magic (law) of cause and effect'. That means that we can be more developed in an area than it seems in our outside life because we have to pay off a karma that disturbs our chance to live the ideal life in that area.

When we decide that we want to be in our ideal Love-Relationship we might have to do something that we haven't done before, or maybe not in this life, in order to create something new that leads us to growth. When we discover that our Love-Relationship is not the ideal, we should ask ourselves: "what can I do to improve it"?

> "WE ARE BORN WITH DIFFERENT PERSONALITIES AND ABILITIES AND THEREFORE WE ARE RAISED DIFFERENTLY, EVEN WITH THE SAME PARENTS, BUT IF WE HAVE THE DESIRE, WE ARE WILLING TO WORK TOWARDS A SUCCESSFUL AND IDEAL LOVE-RELATIONSHIP."
>
> Shantiom Mumtaz Mahal

First study the three different categories of babies and ask yourself: Which category of babies did I belong to? Be also aware of that you can be more or less developed in different areas and at different times of your life too.

- **THE INFLUENCED BABY**
  The largest number of babies, with an underdeveloped conscious mind and underdeveloped thought filter.

- **THE MIXED BABY**
  Many babies, with a weak thought filter and/or very developed conscious mind and reasoning, very developed thought filter.

- **THE AWARE BABY**
  Very few babies with strong thought filter, very developed conscious mind and reasoning, very developed thought filter.

Chapter 2

THE INFLUENCED BABY

Most babies with underdeveloped conscious mind and underdeveloped thought filter.

These children take most of the outside information and paradigms into their subconscious mind and make them their own paradigms (multitude of habits).

(Outside information, behaviour and paradigms (multitude of habits), family, media etc.)

Children with less developed parents	Children with more developed parents
These children live basically on the outside information they get and do what everybody else tells and shows them to do, which keeps them underdeveloped and very close to underdeveloped animals if they don't learn to think of what they do. They will easily become followers of the follower and come into blame-games with other people.	These children begin to think and reason about the information and stimulation they get which make them become more developed and aspire for their own identity and further development. They can go as far as all the information and stimulation they receive. All children have the possibility to develop to the highest awareness.

SPIRITUAL, SOUL-LEVEL

CONSCIOUS, THINKING MIND-LEVEL

SUBCONSCIOUS, EMOTIONAL MIND-LEVEL

BODY-LEVEL

THE MIXED BABY

Many babies with weak thought filter and/or very developed conscious mind and reasoning, very developed thought filter. Nowadays many babies are only taking in some of the outside information they want to think about and neglecting other things that they don't want and need for their development. The children are weak at some levels of understanding and thinking and are very strong in some other levels of understanding and thinking.

(Outside information, behaviour and paradigms (multitude of habits), family, media etc.)

Children with less developed parents

If the parents and people around the children don't allow the children to think for themselves the result may be that the children get set-backs in their development and they become just as weak or weaker than their parents.

Children with more developed parents

If the children get a chance to continue their creative state of mind the result will probably be very creative, imaginative and inventive children.

They can go very far in developing a rich outer and inner life.

(Diagram labels: SPIRITUAL, SOUL-LEVEL; CONSCIOUS, THINKING MIND-LEVEL; SUBCONSCIOUS, EMOTIONAL MIND-LEVEL; BODY-LEVEL)

Chapter 2

THE AWARE BABY

Very few babies with strong thought filter, very developed conscious mind and reasoning, very developed thought filter. These children don't accept all the outside information and paradigms (multitude of habits), they start to think, reason and select information very early.

(Outside information, behaviour and paradigms (multitude of habits), family, media etc.)

Children with less developed parents	Children with more developed parents
Outside and inside karma (exchanges) and circumstances can hold the children back in their development although they can be born with a very aware conscious thinking mind.	The children have the potential to create wonders both for themselves and others and develop these while they choose not to look at hindrances as problems they look only for solutions and that can result in children that become masters both here on earth and beyond faster than the other baby-types.
	All children have the possibility to develop to the highest awareness.

(Diagram labels: SPIRITUAL, SOUL-LEVEL; CONSCIOUS, THINKING MIND LEVEL; SUBCONSCIOUS, EMOTIONAL MIND-LEVEL; BODY-LEVEL)

THE SEVEN LEVELS OF AWARENESS

The seven levels of awareness are at the top of 'The magic (law) of perpetual transmutation' and 'The magic (law) of perpetual increase'.

This pyramid represents humans as the top of the creation and the different developmental stages humans experience in different areas of their life before they master what they are doing or can do when all the karmas (exchanges of give and receive) are paid off.

Only a perfect living Soul-Master can help his disciples to pay off karmas: he helps his disciples to release their karmic burden so that the disciple can develop his/her awareness.

THE SEVEN LEVELS OF AWARENESS

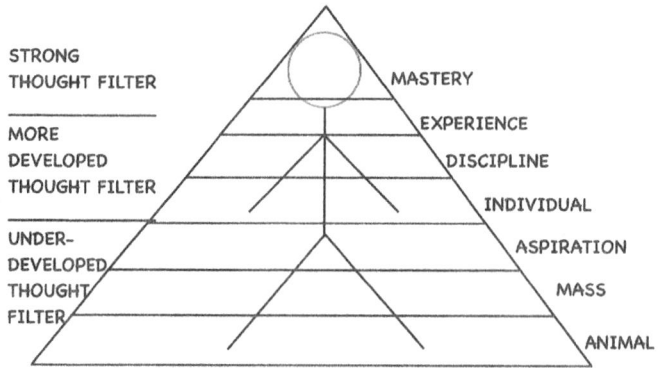

THE HUMAN AND THE UNIVERSE, AS IT IS IN A SMALL HUMAN SO IT IS IN THE BIG UNIVERSE, THE HUMAN CONSISTS OF A SMALL UNIVERSE CONNECTED TO THE BIG UNIVERSE

Thought filter means how much we are consciously aware of, where we get our thoughts from, and how much we accept as our own thoughts and other beings thoughts, and it can both be due to karma and level of awareness.

IT'S ALSO ABOUT HOW MUCH WE CHOOSE TO ACCEPT OR REJECT.

EVERYBODY HAS THE ABILITY TO DEVELOP AN IDEAL LOVE-RELATIONSHIP

All categories of babies have the ability to develop their ideal Love-Relationship. Ask yourself, and be very honest with yourself, was I mostly an 'An influenced baby' or 'A mixed baby' or 'An aware baby'? WE CAN BE DIFFERENT IN DIFFERENT AREAS AND TIMES OF OUR LIVES TOO.

'The magic (law) of cause and effect', also called 'The magic (law) of karma' (exchanges of give and receive) plays a major role in what we experience.

Was my parents' behaviour more or less developed than my ideal? What were my parents' paradigms and what did I copy? What became my paradigms (multitude of habits)?

Whatever we experience we never should feel inferior to anybody else, it's just a learning process we go through.

MY BABYHOOD

What were the paradigms that I was surrounded by and that I grew accustomed to and adapted as my own paradigms (multitude of habits) ???

Make a heart similar to this and exercise your memory.

When you know consciously where your habits come from you can more easily accept or reject things that you need or don't need today, then you are consciously aware of what may stop you or what may help you to move forward in your development and your awareness.

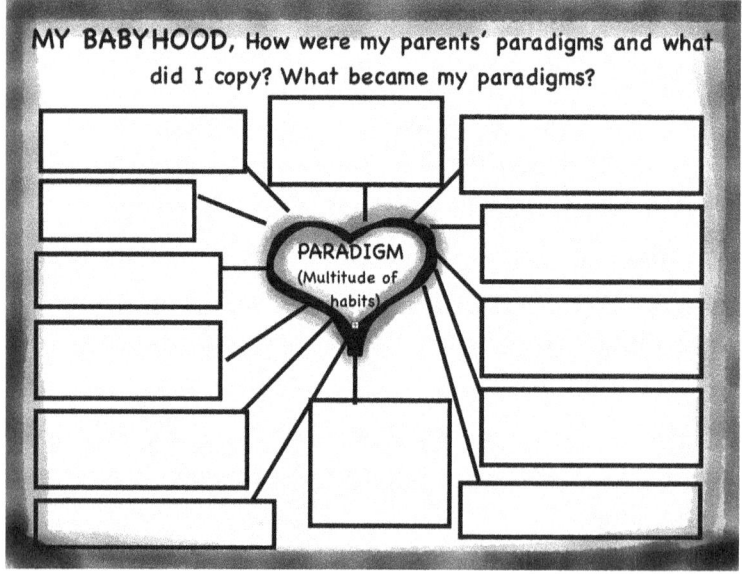

We always express ourselves from inside and out the more genuine and authentic we become. The closer to our natural Comfort Zone we become.

"OUR PARADIGMS BIND US TO THE OPPORTUNITY AND LIMIT THE THOUGHTS THAT WE CHOOSE TO ORIGINATE."

BOB PROCTOR

"YOU CAN ONLY MOVE AHEAD BY LETTING GO OF OLD IDEAS."

BOB PROCTOR

 # CHAPTER 3

HEALING OF THE HEART

<u>THE EXERCISES OF THE HEART WILL HELP US HEAL OUR HEART AND MOVE OUT OF OUR FALSE COMFORT ZONE INTO OUR TRUE COMFORT ZONE WHERE WE CAN REST COMFORTABLY AND USE IT AS A BASE BEFORE WE CREATE OUR IDEAL LOVE-RELATIONSHIP.</u>

The healing of the heart also means that we are working with our heart chakra and that also include healing through time. We can actually become more efficient human beings and more productive and active as well when we let go of old guilt feelings and judgements pointing to ourselves and others. I have learned that when we point one finger at a person we point three fingers towards ourselves, try it and you will see!

There is a certain order in the following exercises and the reason for that is that we shall heal our hearts as efficiently and thoroughly as possible.

- WHEN WE USE THE FIRST HEART WE ONLY SCRATCH THE SURFACE BEFORE WE BEGIN TO DIG DEEPER BY THINKING ABOUT WHAT WE DON'T LIKE.

- WE USE THE SECOND HEART WHEN WE HAVE RECOGNIZED WHAT WE DON'T LIKE AND WE HAVE DISCOVERED THAT WE HAVE REACTIONS TO SOME

OF THE SEVEN NEGATIVE EMOTIONS: FEAR, HATRED, GREED, JEALOUSY, ANGER REVENGE AND SUPERSTITION AND WE WANT TO HEAL THE EMOTIONS BY FORGIVING BOTH OURSELVES AND OTHERS.

WE CAN AT TIMES GET THE FEELING THAT WE HAVE OPENED WOUNDS AFTER DISCOVERING NEGATIVE EMOTIONS, AND WE CAN EVEN GET THE FEELING THAT EVERY THING IS STANDING STILL WHILE WE ADJUST TO THE NEW AND HEALTHIER SELF AND LIFE.

- WE USE THE THIRD HEART WHEN WE ARE READY TO WRITE DOWN EACH EXPERIENCE THAT WE ARE GRATEFUL FOR.

THIS EXERCISE HELPS US TO BE GRATEFUL FOR THE GOOD THAT WE HAVE EXPERIENCED AND FOR WHAT WE HAVE AND THE HEART HEALS ITSELF AFTER WE LET GO OF THE NEGATIVE FEELINGS THAT HAVE BEEN UPSETTING US. THEY HAVE BEEN THERE AS A BLOCK IN OUR SYSTEM, STOPPING US FROM LIVING A BETTER LIFE.

- WE USE THE FOURTH HEART WHEN WE HAVE MADE ALL THE PREPARATIONS AND PASSED THROUGH AND HEALED OUR PAST NEGATIVE EXPERIENCES IN OUR FALSE COMFORT ZONE AND LEFT IT FOR OUR TRUE COMFORT ZONE AND WE ARE READY TO PLAN VIVIDLY OUR IDEAL LOVE-RELATIONSHIP AND LIFE.

Chapter 3

Now let's think about what you didn't like about your childhood. Make a heart like the picture here in the book and write as a headline:

THINGS THAT I DIDN'T LIKE ABOUT MY CHILDHOOD

Remember that we don't do this to accuse our parents, we should rather forgive them and ourselves.

But, let all the negative emotions come up to the surface and face them courageously. The negative emotions are: Fear, hatred, greed, jealousy, anger, revenge and superstition.

Watch yourself react to what you didn't like.

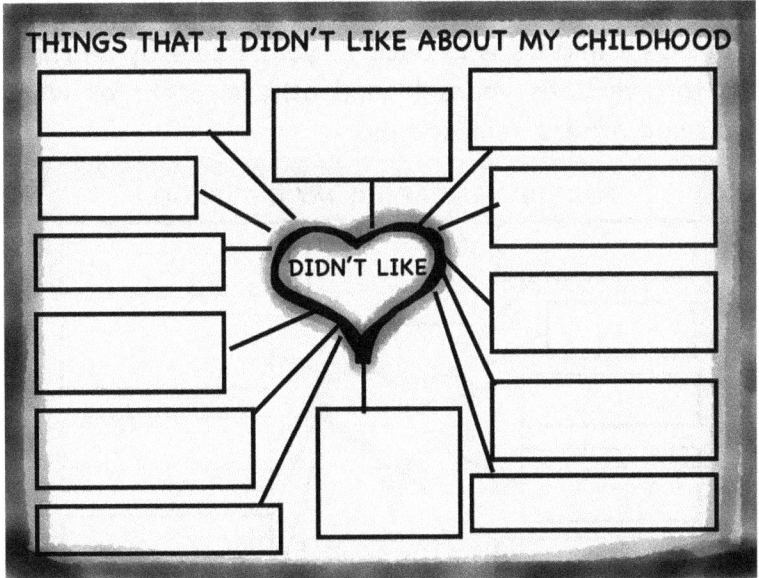

Fill in the most important things you didn't like about your childhood and don't be shy but honest with yourself!

FORGIVENESS ABOUT MY CHILDHOOD

When we have disliked something we ourself have experienced or together with somebody else, where either somebody's or our own behaviour has affected us, it is very good to learn to forgive that person or ourselves. Then we say three times (and write if we want): I forgive you (or myself) for having said or treated me this way _____ so that it affected me this way _____ despite it isn't true.

I forgive myself for having reacted this way _____. I am now free to move on with a peaceful mind.

This a very good exercise to let go of resentment which is a mixture of disappointment, anger and fear.

Let LOVE find it's way back to your heart by learning to forgive both yourself and others, both for what you and others said and did.

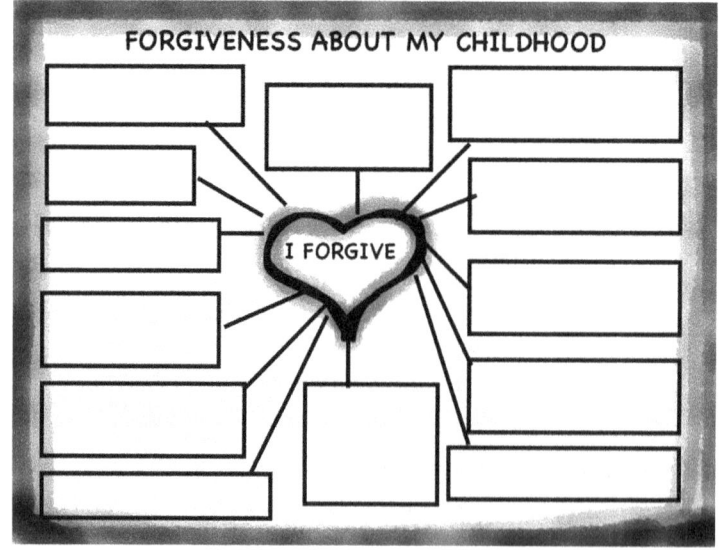

If you need to empty yourself of more things please keep on making new hearts.

Chapter 3

Now let's think about what you liked about your childhood.

Make a heart like the picture here in the book and write as a headline:

THINGS THAT I LIKED ABOUT MY CHILDHOOD

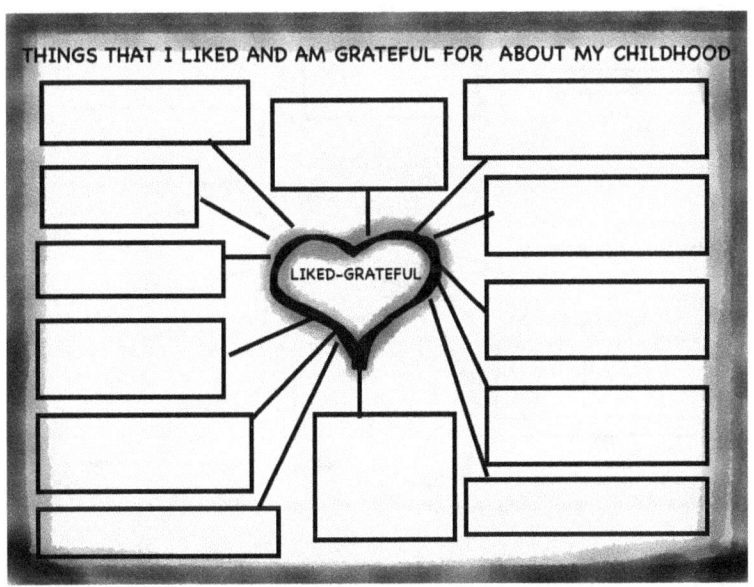

Fill in the most important things you liked about your childhood.

Now we have sorted out what was heavy for us and what was easy for us. Reread it as long as you need it before you proceed.

If you had difficulties figuring out what baby category you belonged to this exercise can help you.

MY IDEAL CHILDHOOD

CREATE YOUR OWN EXCLUSIVE STORY ABOUT HOW YOU WOULD HAVE LOVED TO LIVE AS A CHILD WHERE YOU HAD ALL YOUR DESIRES FULFILLED.

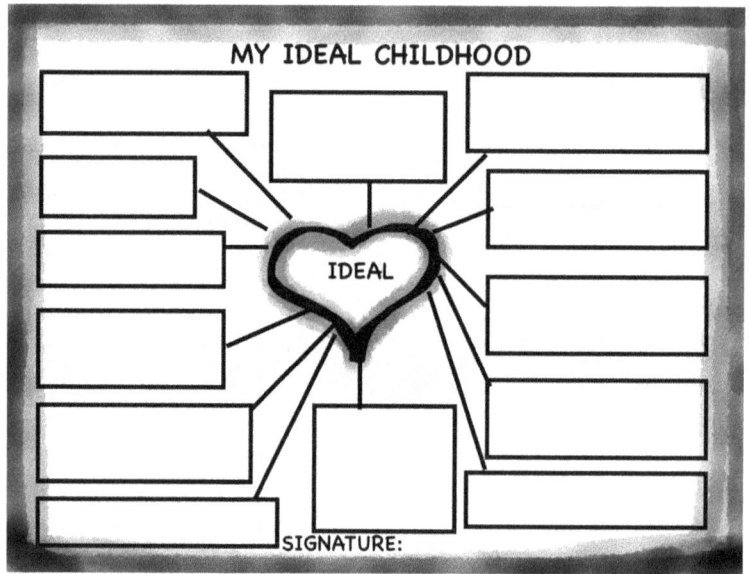

Fantasize vividly about your ideal childhood! Have fun while creating your ideal childhood! What did you long for?

What we longed for as children we often want to give ourselves and/or our children later in life to fulfil our desires.

Ask yourself; What are my hidden desires?

OBSERVE! This is not the same as this is the right childhood for your own children, but a lot of it or maybe most of it could be, there we have to use our own reasoning due to 'The magic (law) of cause and effect' and also give our children the freedom to choose what they desire.

Chapter 3

THINGS THAT I DIDN'T LIKE ABOUT MY YOUTH

Remember that we don't make this to accuse our parents or others, we should rather forgive them and ourselves. But, let all the negative emotions come up to the surface and face them courageously. The negative emotions are: Fear, hatred, greed, jealousy, anger, revenge and superstition.

Here you find things that you had forgotten about a long time ago, but if there are something that bothers you you might get it out of your system by reacting to it and thinking about it until you are tired of reacting to it and you finally want to move forward to a new and more positive version of yourself and then you are ready to step out of your false comfort zone into your true comfort zone before you make a new move towards your ideal Love-Relationship.

FORGIVENESS ABOUT MY YOUTH

When we have disliked something we ourselves have experienced or together with somebody else, where either somebody's or our own behaviour has affected us, it is very good to learn to forgive that person or ourselves. Then we say three times (and write if we want): I forgive you (or myself) for having said or treated me this way _____ so that it affected me this way _____ despite it isn't true.

I forgive myself for having reacted this way _____.
I am now free to move on with a peaceful mind.

This a very good exercise to let go of resentment which is a mixture of disappointment, anger and fear.

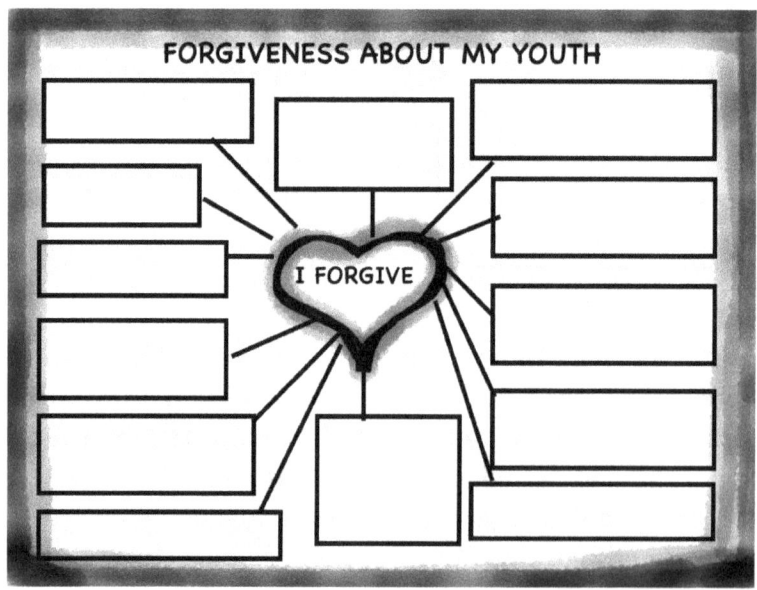

Let LOVE find it's way back to your heart by learning to forgive both yourself and others, both for what you and others said and did.

Chapter 3

THINGS THAT I LIKED ABOUT MY YOUTH

Fill in the most important things you liked about your youth and if you need more hearts make them! Now we have sorted out what was heavy for us and what was easy for us. Reread it as long as you need it before you proceed.

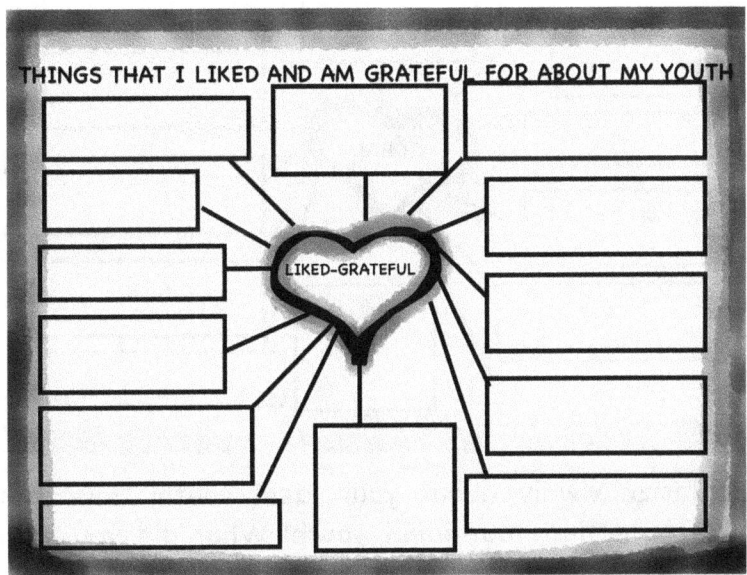

In general we don't have a problem with what we like, but we can become more inspired by our own experiences so that we later on can create our ideal Love-Relationship more easily. And we can also try to create a more beautiful childhood as well as youth for our children based on our own experiences. To be inspired of all the good that we already have experienced is a good encouragement when we are feeling down knowing that we actually have experienced something good too.

MY IDEAL YOUTH

Create your own exclusive story about how you would have loved to live as a youngster and where you had all your desires fulfilled.

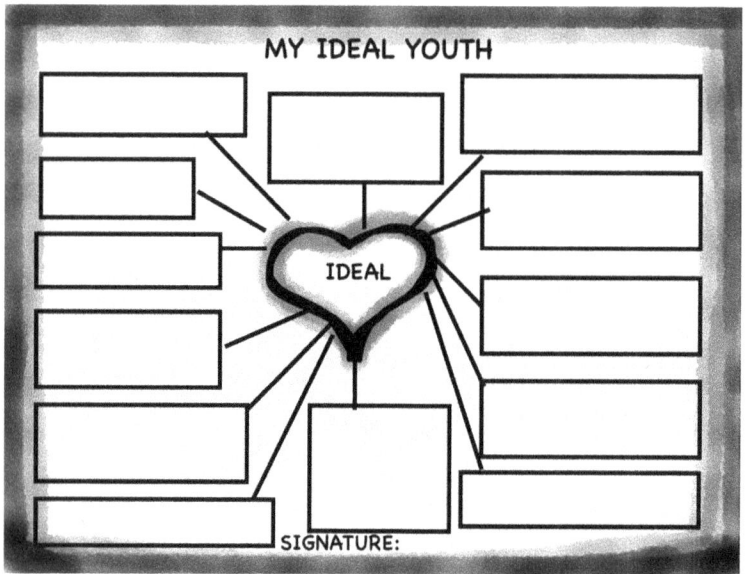

Fantasize vividly about your ideal youth! Have fun while creating your ideal youth! What did you long for?

What we longed for as youngsters we often want to give ourselves and/or our children later in life to fulfil our desires. Ask yourself; What are my hidden desires?

OBSERVE! This is <u>not</u> the same as this is the right youth for your own children, but a lot of it or maybe most of it could be, there we have to use our own reasoning due to 'The magic (law) of cause and effect' and also give our children the freedom to choose what they desire.

Chapter 3

THINGS THAT I DIDN'T LIKE ABOUT MY PAST LOVE-RELATIONSHIP(S)

If you have had any Love-Relationship(s) in this life it's well worth reflecting upon it/them and if you remember any in past lives it can be helpful too. Don't force yourself to remember your past lives either you can or you can't, they will come in their own time. Write down everything that upsets you, makes you angry, unhappy, sad or just didn't work.

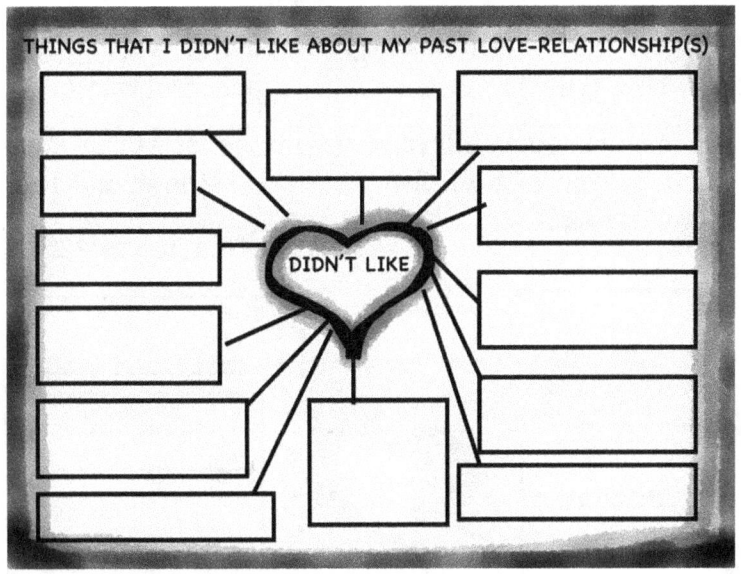

The seven negative emotions – fear, hatred, greed, jealousy, anger, revenge, superstition – can have a very negative impact on us, even on our bodies and it's very healthy to be aware of them even if we suppress them and internalize them so that we can heal them. Be honest and dig deep within you!

AND be aware of your own FEELINGS.

FORGIVENESS ABOUT MY PAST LOVE-RELATIONSHIP(S)

When we have disliked something we ourself have experienced or together with somebody else, where either somebody's or our own behaviour has affected us, it is very good to learn to forgive that person or ourselves. Then we say three times (and write if we want): I forgive you (or myself) for having said or treated me this way _____ so that it affected me this way _____ despite it isn't true.

I forgive myself for having reacted this way_____.
I am now free to move on with a peaceful mind.

This a very good exercise to let go of resentment which is a mixture of disappointment, anger and fear.

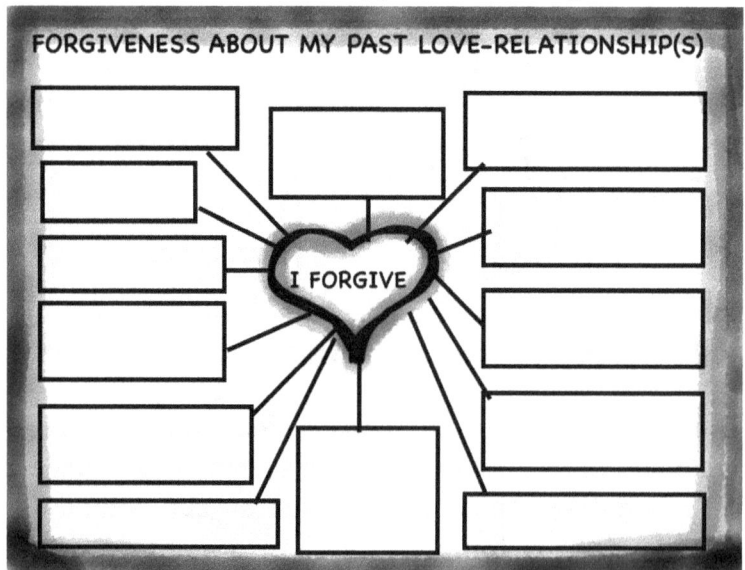

Let LOVE find it's way back to your heart by learning to forgive both yourself and your past Love-Relationship(s), both for what you or he/she said or did to upset you.

Chapter 3

THINGS THAT I LIKED ABOUT MY PAST LOVE-RELATIONSHIP(S)

Fill in the most important things you liked about your past Love-Relationship(s) and if you need more hearts make them! Now we have sorted out what was heavy for us and what was easy for us.

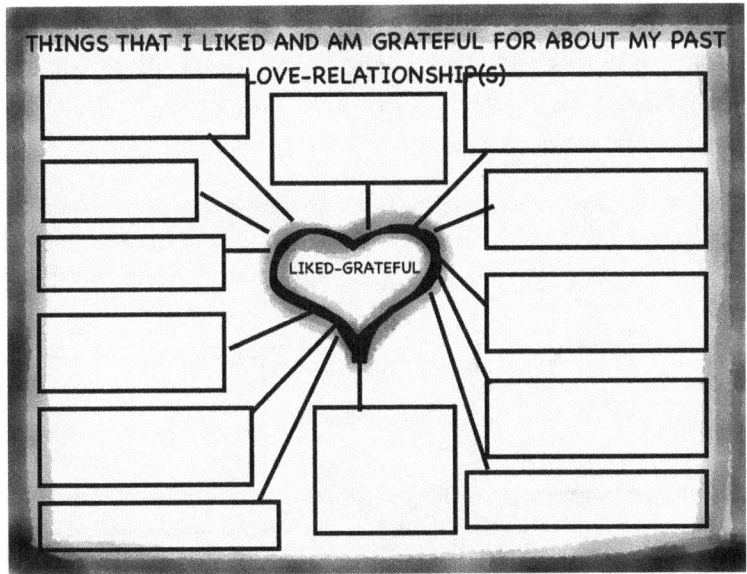

Reread it as long as you need it before you proceed. In general we don't have a problem with what we liked, but we can become more inspired by our own good experiences so that we later on can create our ideal Love-Relationship more easily. To be inspired of all the good that we already have experienced is a good reminder when we are feeling down knowing that we actually have experienced something good too.

THINGS THAT I DON'T LIKE ABOUT MY PRESENT LOVE-RELATIONSHIP

If you are in a Love-Relationship and it's well worth reflecting upon it and whether you believe that you can improve it or not it can still be valuable to give it some investigation and reflect upon it to learn more and heal yourself.

Write down everything that you don't like, upsets you, makes you angry, unhappy, sad or just didn't or don't work and use several hearts if necessary.

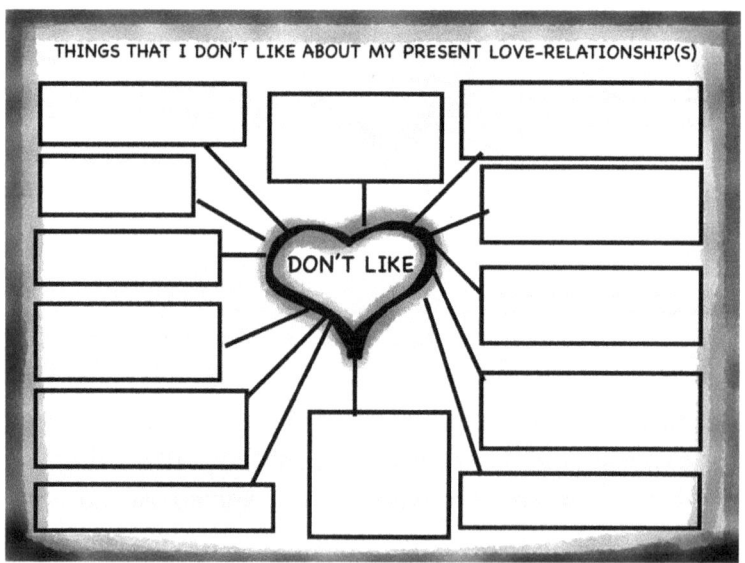

The seven negative emotions: fear, hatred, greed, jealousy, anger, revenge, superstition, can have a very negative impact on us, even on our bodies and it's very healthy to be aware of them even if we suppress them and internalize them, and be aware of your own feelings so that we can heal them. Be honest and dig deep within you!

Chapter 3

FORGIVENESS ABOUT MY PRESENT LOVE-RELATIONSHIP

When we have disliked something we ourself have experienced or together with somebody else, where either somebody's or our own behaviour has affected us, it is very good to learn to forgive that person or ourselves. Then we say three times (and write if we want): I forgive you (or myself) for having said or treated me this way _____ so that it affected me this way _____ despite it isn't true.

I forgive myself for having reacted this way _____.
I am now free to move on with a peaceful mind.

This a very good exercise to let go of resentment which is a mixture of disappointment, anger and fear.

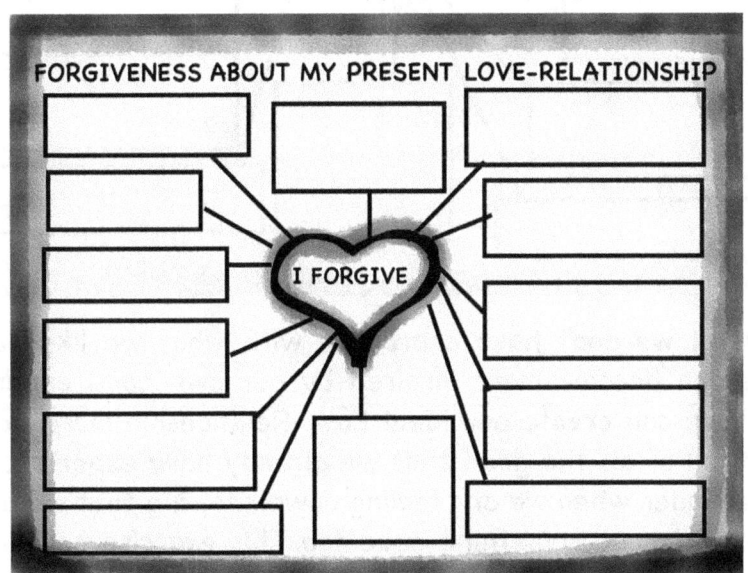

Let LOVE find it's way back to your heart by learning to forgive both yourself and your ongoing Love-Relationship, both for what you or he/she said or did/does to upset you.

THINGS THAT I LIKE ABOUT MY PRESENT LOVE-RELATIONSHIP

Fill in the things you like and are grateful for about your present Love-Relationship and if you need more hearts make them! Now we have sorted out what was heavy for us and what was easy for us.

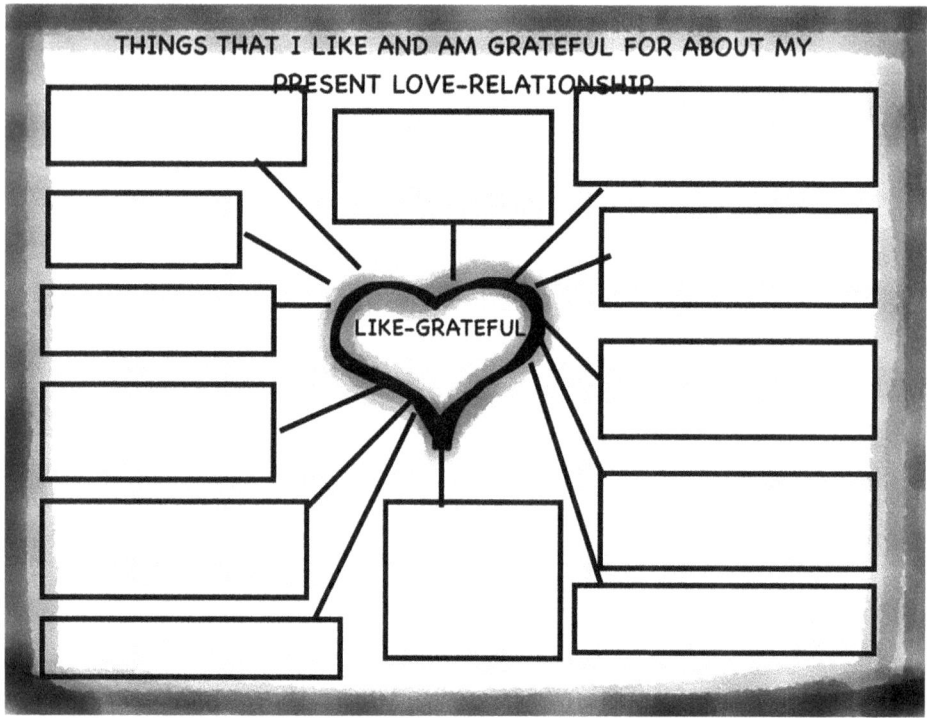

In general we don't have a problem with what we liked or like, but we can become more inspired by our own good experiences so that we can create our ideal Love-Relationship more easily. To be inspired of all the good that we already have experienced is a good reminder when we are feeling down knowing that we actually have experienced something good too. This exercise can help you to appreciate your present Love-Relationship and maybe turn it into an ideal Love-Relationship.

> "GET THE BASIC IDEAS IN PLACE AND GET MOVING."
>
> BOB PROCTOR

"IT IS BETTER TO STEP FORWARD INTO GROWTH RATHER THAN STEP BACKWARD INTO SAFETY."

BOB PROCTOR

 # CHAPTER 4

THE IDEAL LOVE-RELATIONSHIP AS OUR GOAL IN A GREATER PERSPECTIVE
THE SOUL = THE SCIENCE OF UNIVERSAL LIVING

'The magic (law) of perpetual transmutation' and 'The magic (law) of perpetual increase', The universal process on earth, The human process on earth–The seven levels of awareness.

Now I am going to share with you some of The Science Of Universal Living:

THE
SCIENCE
OF
UNIVERSAL
LIVING   = THE SOUL

We want to investigate how our life works in alignment with the universal magics (laws) so that we can better understand why things are happening as they do and what we create in our mind actually comes out as results at a later point in time if we are emotionally involved with the idea.

Therefore it is well worth our investment in time to make a decision to create our IDEAL LOVE-RELATIONSHIP.

When we want to create our GOAL it helps us to be at a harmonious place where we can be inspired to listen to our Soul and be inspired from within to find out our desires and create our ideal Love-Relationship.

There is a universal magic (law) called 'The magic (law) of perpetual transmutation', this magic (law) is about things and beings going from one form to the next in a flow that strives upwards in evolution. For example, a light candle goes from a solid candle to gas.

The under magic (law) is 'The magic (law) of perpetual increase' and that tells us how we naturally strive for higher awareness and that starts from the plants and trees and moves upward through reptiles, fish, insects and snakes, further through fowls and mammals up to the human state.

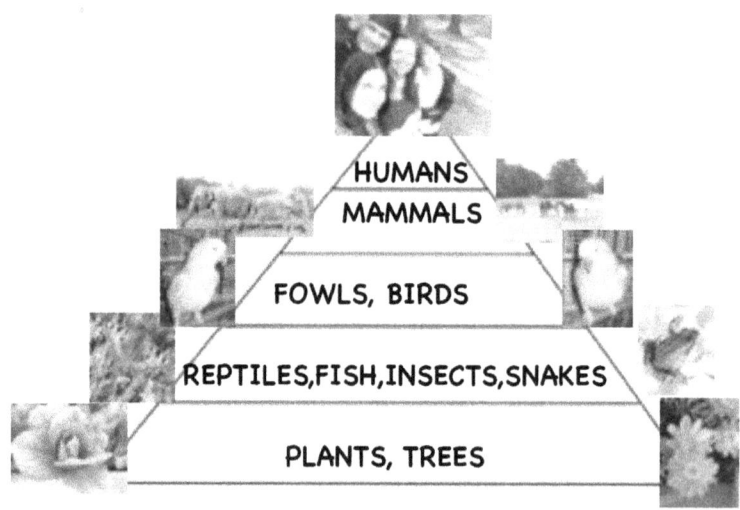

THE UNIVERSAL PROCESS ON EARTH

Chapter 4

THE UNIVERSAL PROCESS ON EARTH

The universe is constantly creating and energy is forever moving into form, through form and dissolving before it moves back into form.

A star is born, another dies.

On earth, lifeforms (souls) go from one body to another body in a reincarnation cycle. All living things that we see in the world can be divided into five groups. Human life is the highest form of creation.

Generally we move into a higher form of life.

From the bottom of the pyramid as here described:

- Plants are at the bottom of the pyramid. They are at the lowest level of understanding in life. They can't move from place to place, but they do communicate on their level of understanding.
- Reptiles, fish, insects and snakes are at the second level of understanding. They are not as smart as birds.
- Birds and fowl are at the third level of understanding. Although they can fly freely they are not as smart as mammals.
- Mammals are at the fourth level of understanding.

  They are lower in understanding than humans because they can't understand that they are souls connected with divine love.
- Humans are at the fifth level of understanding. We can understand that we are souls and a part of the divine love and not only actors in our own lives. This is the top of the pyramid and the highest form of life in the universe and creation. THE GOAL: The goal for all souls is to become humans-the highest form of creation.

With respect, understanding and love for each form of life, all forms will eventually become humans. Going and passing from one form to the next, in countless lifetimes. Generally when we have learned the lessons on one step we have learned enough to move up to the next level of awareness of the lifeforms.

There are however some individuals that make quantum leaps and also those who have a lesson to learn by degrading themselves in awareness.

COMPARISON OF THE VALUE OF LIVES AT THE DIFFERENT LEVELS OF LIFE

- IF YOU PLUCK SOMEBODY'S FLOWERS, THEY WILL YELL AT YOU.
- IF YOU STEEL A HEN FROM THE FARMER, HE WILL ASK YOU TO PAY FOR IT.
- IF YOU STEEL A HORSE FROM THE FARMER, YOU WILL GET A TICKET FROM THE AUTHORITIES.
- IF YOU KILL THE FARMER, YOU WILL GO TO JAIL.

Now you probably wonder why I am telling you this and what this has to do with our ideal Love-Relationship, but this is a background describing the value at the different levels of development why even the tiniest little flower strives to grow towards the sun and every living being is striving for more, to be more, live more, to have more and to do more and new goals all the time and among them THE IDEAL LOVE-RELATIONSHIP.

Chapter 4

THE HEALTHY NATURAL HUMAN PROCESS IN LIFE

Humans are, like the universe, constantly creating.

We tap into the higher side of our own personality, the spiritual world, and we bring it into the intellectual (thinking), emotional, physical, social, material and environmental world.

Knowing is not enough to get results.

Results come from behaviour and behaviour is caused by our paradigms (multitude of habits). That's why it is important for us to create new paradigms all the time, so that we can grow in awareness and become masters of our own lives. As humans we go from the animal state of being and learn gradually to use our higher faculties of the mind.

There are however some individuals that make quantum leaps and also those who have a lesson to learn by degrading themselves in awareness and sometimes masters choose to come to us in different forms to teach us. You can't look at people's bodies or outside life to determine how far they are in their development, that is only showing their history.

Everybody is rich, healthy, wealthy and loving in potential.

WE ARE NATURALLY GOAL SEEKING, GOAL ORIENTED

We are naturally striving for the better.

Everyone will be inspired to reach the top of the pyramid, to move into a higher form/level of ourself into abundance of harmonious
LOVE.

THE SEVEN LEVELS OF AWARENESS

And when we go further in the evolution and we are humans, we strive for even higher ideals than the other life forms on earth. Humans use the higher faculties of their minds to gain higher awareness and that's where we take the top off **'THE UNIVERSAL PROCESS ON EARTH' PYRAMID,** which are the humans described in 'The seven levels of awareness' pyramid where we show the details of the human evolution:

THE HUMAN PROCESS ON EARTH in 'THE SEVEN LEVELS OF AWARENESS'.

THE SEVEN LEVELS OF AWARENESS

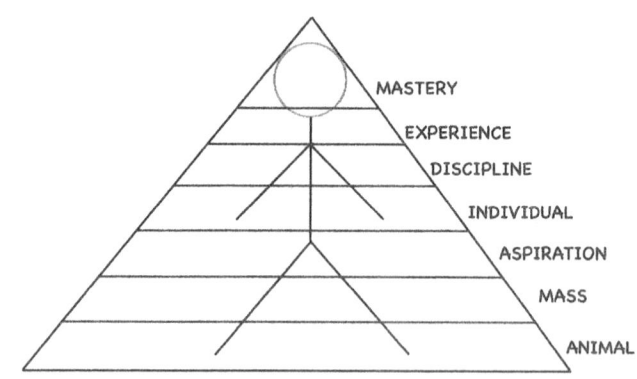

THE HUMAN AND THE UNIVERSE, AS IT IS IN A SMALL HUMAN SO IT IS IN THE BIG UNIVERSE, THE HUMAN CONSISTS OF A SMALL UNIVERSE CONNECTED TO THE BIG UNIVERSE

Chapter 4

THE SEVEN LEVELS OF AWARENESS DESCRIBED FROM THE BOTTOM UPWARDS:

- **ANIMAL AWARENESS, FIGHT OR FLIGHT**
  When we become humans for the first time we mostly come from an animal life, so animal behaviour is still a part of us. We act and react with their instincts without thinking. That's how most animals act, except for those that are more developed. Many humans are at the same level as most animals, they act and react without really thinking why they do that and how they can improve themselves.

- **MASS AWARENESS, FOLLOW THE FOLLOWER**
  The second level of awareness is to follow a follower. That's in general what most people do. They just go where the masses are going and that doesn't always lead to the best results they want. They just go on in the same patterns as they always did, follow the follower. People get "hypnotized" by each other as if under mass hypnosis.

- **ASPIRATION, BREAKING OUT OF THE BOX**
  We aspire to something higher than the masses, we want to rise out of the masses and become more of an individual and follow something of a higher nature within ourselves. Often when we have reached that level, we become pulled down by the people at the level of the masses and the animal level who want to keep us in their state of mind,"the box".

- **INDIVIDUAL, THINKING BY OURSELF**
Now we have aspired up to an individual level. We have broken out of the animal state, the mass state and aspired through "the box" to an individual state. We dare to stand up for our own thoughts. We realize that we can think by ourselves.

- **DISCIPLINE, WITH PASSION**
Since we have realised that we can think by ourselves, and that we are an individual on our own, we have the ability to discipline ourselves through our thoughts and feelings. That comes automatically when we want to do something and are emotionally involved and burn for it with passion.

- **EXPERIENCE, RESULTS OF A TRAINED MIND**
When we have the discipline to go through things with our thoughts and feelings and have a burning passion, we have reached the state where we experience the results. That is the results of a trained mind, where we have managed to go through all the stages.

- **MASTERY, CONSCIOUSLY AWARE**
When we consciously can go through and can manage one of the levels of living, we become a master of the mind in that level of living and if we can make it in several levels of living we even become a greater master.

"IN ORDER TO SEE OPPORTUNITY, YOU MUST BE <u>AWARE</u> YOU ARE IN THE RIGHT PLACE AT THE RIGHT TIME."

BOB PROCTOR

"SET A GOAL TO ACHIEVE SOMETHING THAT IS SO BIG, SO EXHILARATING THAT IT EXCITES YOU AND SCARES YOU AT THE SAME TIME. IT MUST BE A GOAL THAT IS SO APPEALING, SO MUCH IN LINE WITH YOUR SPIRITUAL CORE THAT YOU CAN'T GET IT OUT OF YOUR MIND. IF YOU DO NOT GET CHILLS WHEN YOU SET A GOAL, YOU'RE NOT SETTING BIG ENOUGH GOALS."

BOB PROCTOR

CHAPTER 5

THE IDEAL LOVE-RELATIONSHIP AND THE SEVEN MAGIC GOAL STEPS TO SUCCESS-SEEKING MORE OF ALL KINDS!

'The magic (law) of perpetual increase' is the highest level with humans at the top of the pyramid in 'The seven levels of awareness.'

As we climb up to the top of the 'The seven levels of awareness pyramid' we constantly go through 'The seven goal steps to success' on both a smaller scale and a bigger scale.

THE MAGIC OF PERPETUAL INCREASE IS AN UNDER-MAGIC (LAW) OF THE MAGIC OF PERPETUAL TRANSMUTATION.

IT IS THE REFINED RESULT OF LONG AND CONSTANT EFFORT, PERSEVERANCE AND PERSISTENCE TO NEVER, NEVER GIVE UP ON A GOAL THAT LEADS US TO A HIGHER AWARENESS. We can change the ways to get there, but never change our purpose in life.

WE MOVE UPWARDS IN THE POSITIVE, CREATIVE PINGALA CHANNEL.

Our goal is to be so focused and aware that we can move freely and fast between the different levels of living: the spiritual, the thinking (intellectual, conscious) mind, the emotional (subconscious) mind, the body, the social, the material, and the environmental level. Our <u>freedom</u> is <u>awareness</u>!

OUR NEW GAINED <u>AWARENESS</u> IS OUR <u>FREEDOM</u>!

THE SEVEN LEVELS OF LIVING

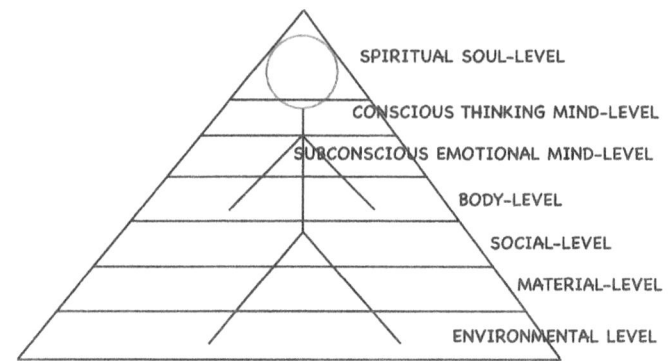

THE HUMAN AND THE UNIVERSE, AS IT IS IN A SMALL HUMAN SO IT IS IN THE BIG
UNIVERSE, THE HUMAN CONSISTS OF A SMALL UNIVERSE CONNECTED TO THE BIG UNIVERSE

THE SEVEN LEVLES OF LIVING

1. Spiritual, Soul-level
2. Conscous, Thinking-Mind Level
3. Subconscous, Emotional Mind-Level
4. Body-Level
5. Social-Level
6. Material-Level
7. Environmental-Level

THE SEVEN LEVELS OF LIVING

THE SEVEN LEVELS OF LIVING ARE DIFFERENT EXPRESSIONS OF ALL THE MAGICS (LAWS), BUT SOME OF THE MAJOR MAGICS (LAWS) ARE: THE MAGIC (LAW) OF PERPETUAL TRANSMUTATION, THE MAGIC (LAW) OF PERPETUAL INCREASE, THE MAGIC (LAW) OF CAUSE AND EFFECT, THE MAGIC (LAW) OF VIBRATION, THE MAGIC (LAW) OF POLARITY, THE MAGIC (LAW) OF THE SOUL, THE LATTER WHEN YOU ARE INITIATED BY A PERFECT LIVING SOUL-MASTER. THE SEVEN LEVELS OF LIVING AS MENTIONED ABOVE ARE EXCHANGES BOTH ON THE INSIDE AND ON THE OUTSIDE.

Chapter 5

MY SOUL-MASTER'S MESSAGE ABOUT THE SEVEN LEVELS OF LIVING.

"I WANT ALL MY DISCIPLES TO HAVE A GOOD LIFE IN ALL SEVEN LEVELS OF LIVING, BUT SOMETIMES WE GO THROUGH KARMAS (EXCHANGES OF GIVE AND RECEIVE) WITHIN 'THE MAGIC (LAW) OF CAUSE AND EFFECT, THAT MAKES IT DIFFICULT TO LIVE IN ALL LEVELS FULLY.

THEN WE SHALL STRIVE TO FULFIL OUR LIVES WHEN THE KARMA IS PAID.

THERE IS NO REASON FOR US NOT TO LIVE A FULFILLED LIFE IN ALL LEVELS OF LIVING, IF WE CAN. IT IS NATURAL FOR HUMANS TO STRIVE FOR PERFECTION IN ALL LEVELS OF LIVING.

THAT'S INCLUDED IN 'THE MAGIC (LAW) OF PERPETUAL TRANSMUTATION' AND 'THE MAGIC (LAW) OF PERPETUAL INCREASE'.

WE WANT TO REACH THE TOP IN ALL LEVELS OF LIVING."

Received telepathically from my perfect living SOUL-MASTER

> We live in seven levels of living in the world. Most of us strive to live conscoiusly in all levels in order to be loving, happy, romantic, healthy, harmonious, intuitive, imaginative, wealthy, strong, faithful, powerful, inspired, goal-oriented and aware among other things and to pay off our karmas and become free from the bonds of the world.

1. SPIRITUAL, SOUL-LEVEL

2. CONSCIOUS, THINKING MIND-LEVEL

3. SUBCONSCIOUS, EMOTIONAL MIND-LEVEL

4. PHYSICAL BODY-LEVEL

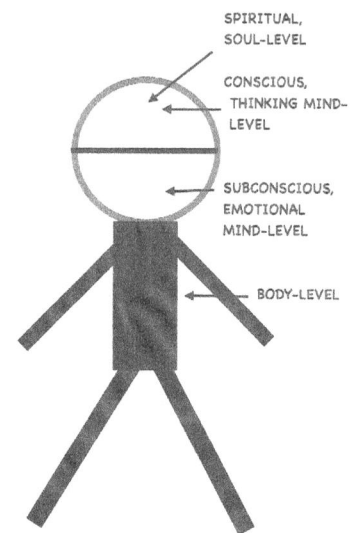

5. SOCIAL-LEVEL, examples and more...

There are several kinds of relation- ships more than those here...

6. MATERIAL-LEVEL, examples and more...

WHEN WE EXPRESS SOMETHING OUTSIDE OF OURSELVES, IT ALWAYS STARTS FROM THE INSIDE AND GOES TO THE OUTSIDE WORLD. FOR EXAMPLE: WE THINK AND THEN WE TALK AND FURTHER MORE WE ACT PHYSICALLY.

But there are other things that matter to our results as well...

The magic (law) of cause and effect is a major magic (law) of the universe and it's even called 'The magic (law) of karma, (which has to do with giving and receiving).

You have to think about every single act that you do also to others will turn back to you and the more advanced and developed you are the more you have to pay. So we should always behave nicely and kindly towards each other. Just the same way as we want to be treated. The magic (law) of cause and effect

7. ENVIRONMENTAL-LEVEL, examples and more...

is spanning over the whole of 'The seven magic goal steps to success' and 'The seven levels of living'.

On every step there may occur something that has to do with 'The magic (law) of cause and effect'. The magic (law) of action and reaction. (GIVE AND RECEIVE)

To simplify it we can say that a goal is created twice, first in our thoughts and then in reality.

When we plan our goal, we plan our actions in reality. LOVE = Remember, if we give LOVE, we shall receive LOVE: If we are kind and patient towards others, other people will be kind and patient towards us.

Chapter 5

> **THE GOLDEN RULE OF SUCCESS =**
> 'AS YOU SOW, SO SHALL YOU REAP'
> 1. ACTION (cause) ➤ 2. REACTION (effect)
> If we put seeds in a rich soil ➤ we harvest richly

Ask yourself: are you the master of your own destiny? There is a saying: 'As you sow, so shall you reap'.

If you want success, this is the golden rule!

Treat yourself with love and respect, and you will also be treated with love and respect, but not always instantly and from the same person, it can come from someone else and also much later. What you send out is the cause and what you receive back is the effect. This magic (law) is very comprehensive, because it concerns everything, all of our relationships, everything from The spiritual the soul, The conscious thinking mind, The subconscious emotional mind, the body, the social life, the material life and the environmental life. What we send out in the form of our thoughts and actions—we receive back as effects and conditions. Know that 'The magic (law) of attraction' even called 'The law of LOVE' is the cause and growth and/or expansion is the effect.

So why is it important to think and do good and our best for ourselves and others... ?

Well, we work for our own future...

'The magic (law) of cause and effect (exchanges of give and receive) and our actions can be divided into three categories:

1. <u>Actions (karmas) in the now</u>

    Here we create certain things in the now and for the future. We do our best and use wisely 'The highest faculties of our mind' and create our own destiny.

    Remember compassion is the highest faculty of the mind. We should act as if this is the only life that we have!

2. <u>Stored actions (karmas)</u>

    When we have had actions in past lives and we have not yet received or paid off the results/the effects because they are stored for us for our future for a better time for us to give or receive.

3. <u>Stored destined actions (karmas)</u>

    Depending on our past lives and our past behaviours, there is a certain destiny in this life that we have to go through. We can either do it willingly or unwillingly and we can either do it smilingly or cryingly and sometimes we do both...

 RELATIONSHIPS ARE EVERYTHING
EVERYTHING CONNECTS AND COMMUNICATES

Chapter 5

LET US HAVE A LOOK AT THE FORMULA FOR THE SEVEN GOAL STEPS TO SUCCESS!

What I give you here is the formula for much more than 'THE IDEAL LOVE-RELATIONSHIP', it's the formula for your whole life in all areas of your life! It's a gift from me to YOU that you actually have chosen consciously by reading this book.

I am going to guide you through step by step how these 'Seven Magic Goal Steps' are working, and I want you to also be aware of that this process works both in a bigger goal-decision perspective and in every day situations when we normally don't think so much and just act by habit because we are so used to make those decisions and receive the gifts. When we act by habit we get things that we are used to in a natural way. It's at those times that gratitude for what we have and where we are in our lives are so precious because we have up to now been working to get what we have and where we are in awareness.

If we are working towards a goal we will go through a certain pattern that can differ a little depending on the lessons and karma (exchanges of give and receive) we have to pay, but I will share the process in general and talk about some pitfalls that we might run into. Up to now we have been working with number 0. The comfort zone and to get to be more authentic with ourselves.

COMPASSION IS THE HIGHEST FACULTY OF THE MIND!

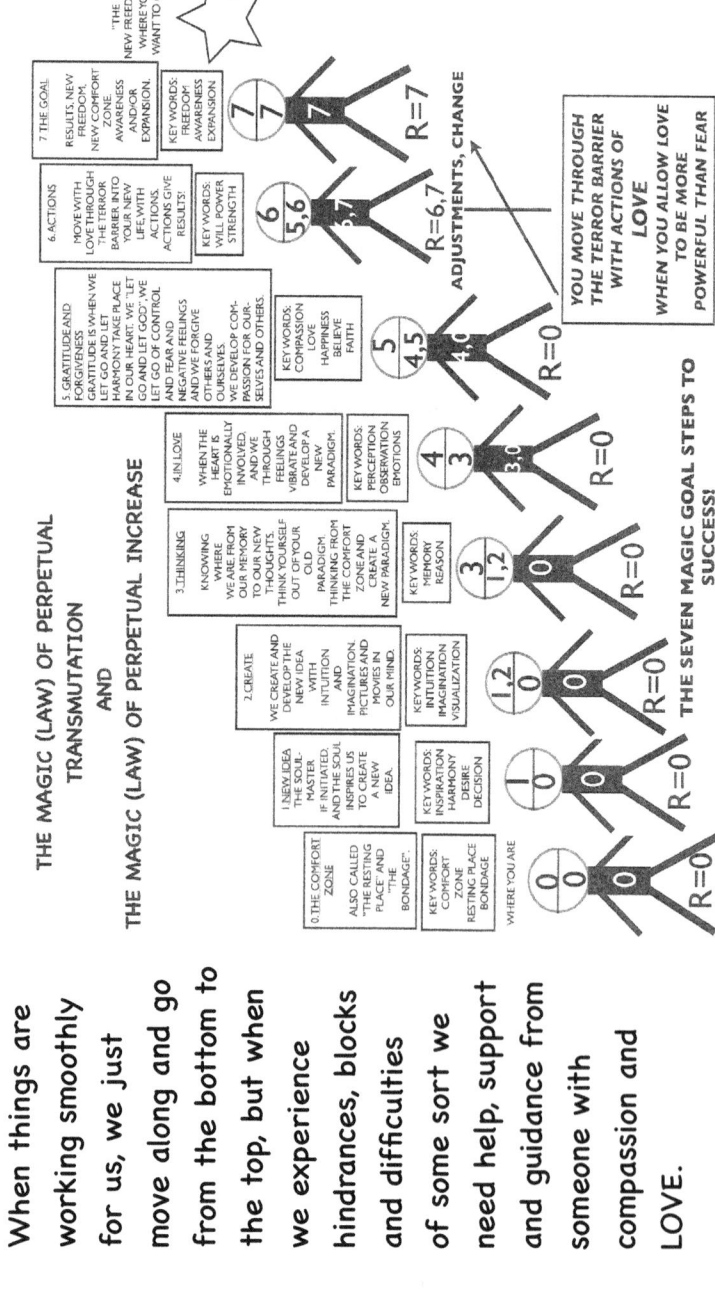

When things are working smoothly for us, we just move along and go from the bottom to the top, but when we experience hindrances, blocks and difficulties of some sort we need help, support and guidance from someone with compassion and LOVE.

Chapter 5

Where it starts: 0. The comfort zone

We have been looking into ourselves and our own experiences in the past, so that we more easily can let go of painful feelings and experiences and forgive both ourselves and others. We have been working with healing of our own heart and by doing that we also learn to forgive others and understand both ourselves and others better. That also in turn gives other people a chance to heal their hearts when we forgive them. We don't even have to talk with them face to face, we can still help both ourselves and others by simply following this process. By having gone through this huge healing process up to now, we can become more happy, productive, released, forgiving, loved as human beings. (we can receive more love, in all levels of living)

Before we move forward in our 'Seven Goal Steps To Success' I am going to explain to you in a very simplified way how 'The Seven Goal Steps To Success' work in the body. They work the same in a greater universal perspective because as it is in the smaller human body it also works the same in a greater perspective in the universe. As it is in the small so it is in the big.

Here within 'The Seven Goal Steps To Success' we experience countless universal magics (laws), but there is one major magic that we have to be extra much aware of and that is 'The magic (law) of cause and effect' even called 'The magic (law) of karma' (exchanges of give and receive).

In 'The seven goal steps to success' we even utilize our 'Seven faculties of the mind' to our best ability.

Now, if you wonder how I know all this, it is because I have studied myself and how I do when I think and develop myself, and I can tell you that you can do the same, you can also study yourself to get to know what is happening with you and to you!

THE SEVEN MAGIC GOAL STEPS TO SUCCESS, SIMPLIFIED and how they work in the body!!!

We have three energy channels, minus, neutral and plus.

THE PROCESS OF THE SEVEN MAGIC GOAL STEPS TO SUCCESS IN THE BODY

Chapter 5

THE POSITIVE CHANNEL IS THE UPWARD GOING CHANNEL PULLING US UP TO A HIGHER AWARENESS.

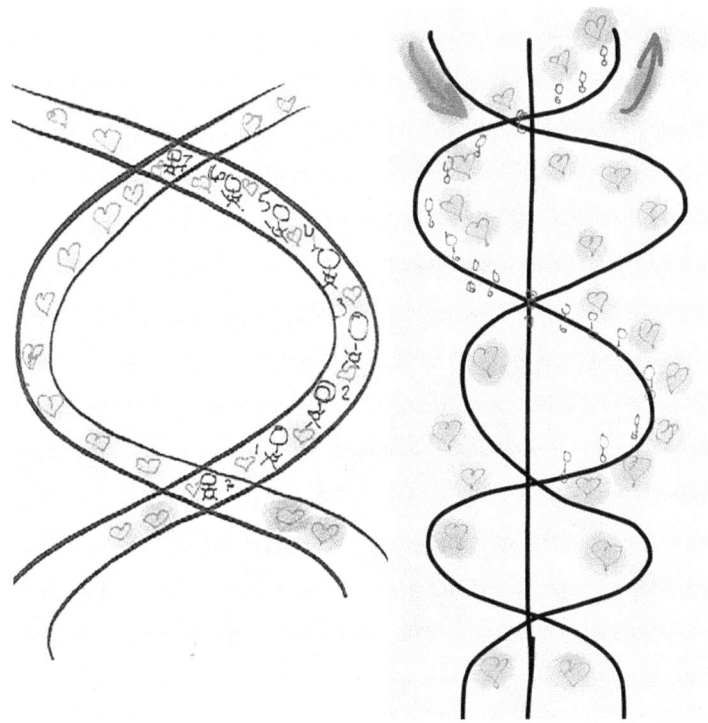

HIGHER AWARENESS

AS WE DEVELOP OUR AWARENESS WE BECOME MORE AND MORE AWARE OF OUR CONSCIOUS THOUGHTS AND HOW THEY AFFECT OUR LIVES.

THE DOWNWARD IDA CHANNEL IS THE NEGATIVE, DESTRUCTIVE, GROUNDING, SLOW-GOING CHANNEL.

THE MIDDLE SUSHUMNA CHANNEL IS THE NEUTRAL HARMONIOUS, SERENE CHANNEL. THE UPWARD PINGALA CHANNEL IS THE POSITIVE, CREATIVE CHANNEL TOWARDS HIGHER AWARENESS, TO THE RIGHT.

HOW WE LIVE IN THE BODY WITH THE SEVEN LEVELS OF LIVING

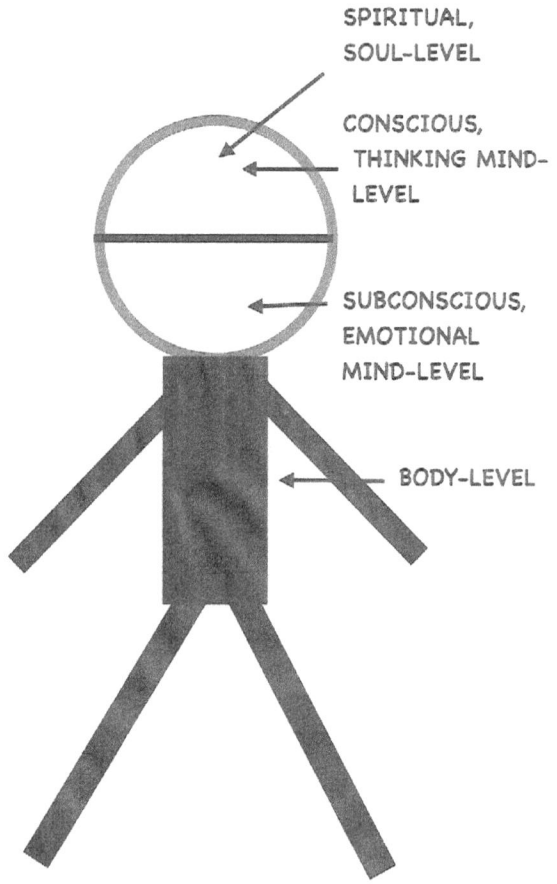

Outside of our body we live in a:

SOCIAL LIFE

MATERIAL LIFE

ENVIRONMENTAL LIFE

Chapter 5

Understand that the power from within is so much stronger and far superior to any circumstance around us.

As you accept a thought, in the upper part of the circle of the mind, called the thinking, conscious mind, it is impressed on the lower part of the circle called the emotional, subconscious mind.

That vibrates into the body and comes out as behaviour or actions in the physical world depending on what we have been thinking of and that in turn gives results.

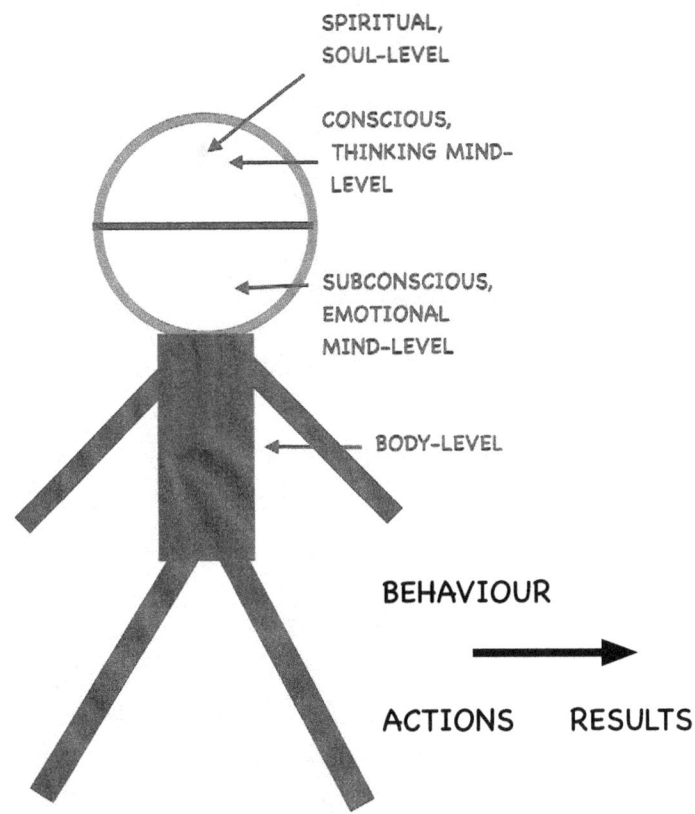

THE SEVEN MAGIC GOAL STEPS TO SUCCESS
— THE WHOLE PROCESS

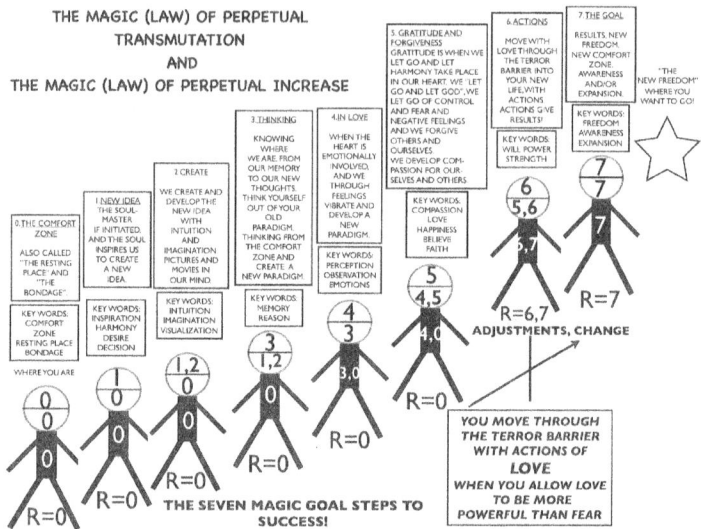

Go back to this pattern and learn subsequently!

THE STEP BY STEP IN DETAILS:

- 0. THE COMFORT ZONE

ALSO CALLED "THE RESTING PLACE" AND "THE BONDAGE".

KEY WORDS: COMFORT ZONE, RESTING PLACE AND BONDAGE

This is where you are, your starting point before you create your new goal. You think 0-COMFORT-ING thoughts, you have 0-COMFORTING feelings and you get the same 0-COMFORTING results all the time. The 0-COMFORTING stands for that there is no change, it stays the same. Wile we are in the comfort zone, also called the resting place and the bondage, we are not ...

Chapter 5

- always aware of that we can stretch for more or something new. We can however in order not to have a false comfort zone work with the heart exercises to release thoughts and feelings from our old paradigm (multitude of habits).

0. THE COMFORT ZONE

ALSO CALLED "THE RESTING PLACE" AND "THE BONDAGE".

KEY WORDS:
COMFORT ZONE
RESTING PLACE
BONDAGE

This figure to the left is a symbol of a human, the head represents and is a symbol of the mind. The upper part of the circle is the conscious and thinking mind and the lower part of the circle is the subconscious and emotional mind.

The 0 stands for the old paradigm, old habits that we hold onto in our mind which results in the same results until we consciously make the decision to change our thoughts which in turn change our feelings which as a result changes our results.

The R = Results

- 1. NEW IDEA

THE SOUL INSPIRES US TO CREATE A NEW IDEA, BUT IF WE ARE INITIATED BY A PERFECT LIVING SOUL-MASTER IT IS HE WHO INSPIRES THE SOUL TO CREATE A NEW IDEA.

KEY WORDS: INSPIRATION, HARMONY, DESIRE AND DECISION.

Now we begin to think 1-NEW IDEA thoughts (new thoughts), but still have 0-COMFORTING feelings and 0-COMFORTING results.

WHAT INSPIRES US? When we are in harmony we get inspired and get in touch with our desires and based upon that we make decisions. Of course our Soul, and Soul-Master if we are initiated, inspire us first of all, but if we choose a calm, serene and inspiring environment and if we are creating a cozy, inspiring atmosphere in our environment, we are very probably more easily inspired to create something new when we surround ourselves with beautiful things, beautiful environment, beautiful people, inside and out. As we have already worked with our comfort zone in our Exercises Of The Heart, we can jump right into our new idea, which is to create our IDEAL LOVE-RELATIONSHIP. So now we have a new Exercise For The Heart!

Chapter 5

The 1 in the figure stands for THE NEW IDEA and the NEW IDEA begins in the conscious, thinking mind, before it moves into form through our emotions in our body and further more into results in the world.

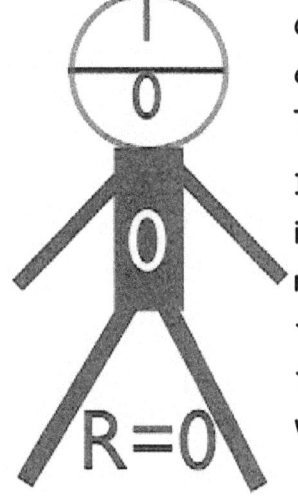

1.NEW IDEA
THE SOUL-MASTER
IF INITIATED, AND THE SOUL INSPIRES US TO CREATE A NEW IDEA.

KEY WORDS:
INSPIRATION
HARMONY
DESIRE
DECISION

The upper part of the circle is the conscious and thinking mind and the lower part of the circle is the subconscious and emotional mind.

The 1 stands for THE NEW IDEA and the 0 stands for the old paradigm, old habits that we hold onto in our mind which results in the same results until we consciously make the decision to change our thoughts which in turn change our feelings which as a result changes our results. The R = Results

If we choose to heal our hearts in the comfort zone, we are more open for the change that takes place when we proceed to our new goal. We start to with both 1 and 2.

NO 7, THE GOAL, MY IDEAL LOVE-RELATIONSHIP

Create your own exclusive, exquisite story about how you would LOVE to live your life with a loved one and have all your desires fulfilled.

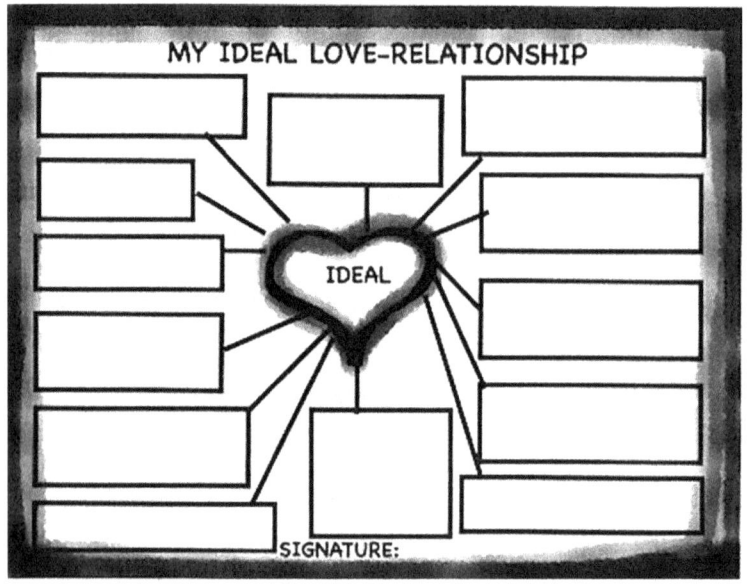

- Fill in your Heart exercise with loving, romantic things that you want to do with your loved one, this makes your heart open for the new that you desire! Read it often!

- 2. CREATE

WE CREATE AND DEVELOP THE NEW IDEA WITH INTUITION AND IMAGINATION. PICTURES AND MOVIES IN OUR MIND.

KEY WORDS: INTUITION, IMAGINATION AND VISUALIZATION.

Chapter 5

RELAX AND GET INSPIRED BY YOUR SOUL AND YOUR SOUL-MASTER (if initiated) WITH INTUITION AND IMAGINATION.

What do you visualize?

What is your desire?

What is your decision?

7, THE GOAL

WHEN WE FILL IN **7 THE GOAL**, WE AUTOMATICALLY USE **1 THE NEW IDEA AND 2 CREATE**, TO CREATE THE GOAL OF OUR DREAMS.

1, NEW IDEA

WE GET INSPIRED IN OUR MIND TO DEVELOP A NEW GOAL, WE GET INSPIRED BY OUR SOUL AND BY THE SOUL-MASTER AS INITIATES. WHEN WE ARE IN HARMONY, WE GET INSPIRED AND GET IN TOUCH WITH OUR DESIRES AND BASED UPON THAT, WE MAKE DECISIONS.

2, CREATE

WE CREATE AND DEVELOP THE NEW IDEA WITH OUR HIGHER FACULTIES OF OUR MIND, **INTUITION AND IMAGINATION**. WHEN WE VISUALIZE OUR NEW GOAL WITH PICTURES AND MOVIES IN OUR MIND, WE DEVELOP OURSELVES AND EXPAND OUR INNER AWARENESS TO A NEW LEVEL, WE GROW!

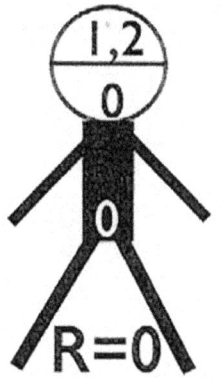

2. CREATE

WE CREATE AND DEVELOP THE NEW IDEA WITH INTUITION AND IMAGINATION. PICTURES AND MOVIES IN OUR MIND.

KEY WORDS:
INTUITION
IMAGINATION
VISUALIZATION

7, THE GOAL

WHEN WE FILL IN 7 THE GOAL, WE AUTOMATICALLY USE 1 THE NEW IDEA AND 2 CREATE, TO CREATE THE GOAL OF OUR DREAMS.

1, NEW IDEA

WE GET INSPIRED IN OUR MIND TO DEVELOP A NEW GOAL, WE GET INSPIRED BY OUR SOUL AND BY THE SOUL-MASTER AS INITIATES. WHEN WE ARE IN HARMONY, WE GET INSPIRED AND GET IN TOUCH WITH OUR HEART'S DESIRES AND BASED UPON THAT, WE MAKE DECISIONS.

WHAT INSIPRES US?

OF COURSE OUR SOUL AND THE SOUL-MASTER INSPIRES US FIRST OF ALL, BUT IF WE CHOOSE A CALM, SERENE AND INSPIRING ENVIRONMENT AND IF WE CREATE A COZY, INSPIRING ATMOSPHERE IN OUR ENVIRONMENT, WE ARE MORE EASILY INSPIRED TO CREATE SOMETHING NEW WHEN WE SURROUND OURSELVES WITH BEAUTIFUL THINGS, BEAUTIFUL ENVIRONMENT, BEAUTIFUL PEOPLE, INSIDE AND OUT.

Chapter 5

2, CREATE - FANTASIZE

WE CREATE AND DEVELOP THE NEW IDEA WITH THE HIGHER FACULTIES OF OUR MIND, <u>INTUITION, DRAW INFORMATION FROM WITHIN AND IMAGINATION, FANTASIZE,</u> WHEN WE VISUALIZE OUR NEW GOAL WITH PICTURES AND MOVIES IN OUR MIND, WE DEVELOP OURSELVES AND EXPAND OUR INNER AWARENESS TO A NEW LEVEL, WE GROW! IT IS VERY IMPORTANT THAT WE DON'T GO AGAINST THE NATURAL MAGICS (LAWS) OF THE UNIVERSE AND TRY TO FORCE SOMETHING TO HAPPEN, THAT NEEDS TIME TO GROW AND DEVELOP UNLESS IT'S KARMA, (EXCHANGES OF GIVING AND RECEIVING) VISUALIZATION NEEDS TO COME TO US NATURALLY. IT CAN COME AS AN INNER PICTURE OR AS AN INNER MOVIE. WHENEVER WE ARE READY FOR IT.

SUCCESS

"ANYONE THAT EVER ACCOMPLISHED ANYTHING, DID NOT KNOW <u>HOW</u> THEY WERE GOING TO DO IT. THEY ONLY KNEW THEY WERE <u>GOING TO DO IT.</u>"

— BOB PROCTOR

"THE IMAGE OF SELF IN YOUR MIND ... CONTROLS THE RESULTS IN YOUR LIFE."

BOB PROCTOR

 CHAPTER 6

THE IDEAL LOVE-RELATIONSHIP AND THE SEVEN MAGIC GOAL STEPS TO SUCCESS! 0, WHERE WE ARE AND 3, THINKING

... AND WE HAVE SPECIAL FOCUS ON BUILDING OUR SELF-IMAGE AND OUR COMMON SELF-IMAGE.

Knowing where you are, from your memory to your new thoughts, you can think yourself out of your old paradigm (multitude of habits).

Think yourself from the comfort zone out of the paradigm (multitude of habits) and go from the old through memory—to the new in your reasoning and create a new paradigm. No matter where you are even if you are alone or in an existing Love-Relationship.

ASK YOURSELF IF YOU ARE IN AN EXISTING LOVE-RELATIONSHIP:

Do I want to stay in this Love-Relationship?

Are we in agreement of working together towards a common ideal Love-Relationship?

When we work on recognizing where we are we explore automatically.

Now we try to go backwards to see where we are, this happens naturally as we try to proceed forward and leave our old paradigm (multitude of habits) before we create a new paradigm. This is a constant ongoing process where we need to update ourselves to get to know where we are at this very moment. When we work on that consciously we can create wonders for ourselves and subsequently others as well.

0, THE COMFORT ZONE

AFTER WE HAVE CREATED OUR NEW GOAL, 7, THE GOAL, WITH THE HELP OF THE STAGE 1, NEW IDEA, AND 2, CREATE, WE MOVE ONTO 0, THE COMFORT ZONE. AND IN ORDER TO KNOW WHERE WE ARE, WE HAVE TO USE STAGE 3, THINKING, WHERE WE USE OUR MEMORY TO KNOW WHERE WE ARE. FOR A WHILE WE HAVE TO THINK IN REVERSE AND REASON TO GET TO KNOW WHERE WE ARE. IT DOESN'T MATTER IF IT IS THE FOUR RULES, WHAT WE EAT, DRINK, HONEST AND MORAL RELATIONSHIPS, SPIRITUAL AWARENESS OR WORLDLY GOALS, WE HAVE TO GO THROUGH THE SAME STAGES. SO WITH THE HELP OF 3, THINKING, WE REMEMBER WHERE WE ARE, OUR COMFORT ZONE, RESTING PLACE AND BONDAGE, WHERE WE START!

Chapter 6

> 3. THINKING
>
> KNOWING WHERE WE ARE, FROM OUR MEMORY TO OUR NEW THOUGHTS. THINK YOURSELF OUT OF YOUR OLD PARADIGM. THINKING FROM THE COMFORT ZONE AND CREATE A NEW PARADIGM.

> KEY WORDS:
> MEMORY
> REASON

3, THINKING

REASON, REASON AND REASON... WE IMPROVE OURSELVES AND OUR LOVE-RELATIONSHIP BY REASONING.

We think in our conscious, thinking mind, reason and create a new paradigm.

Before we created it in our dreams and imagination in a more intuitive way, now we reason about it and think in a more concrete, dense way. we are, we can let go use all the good think will benefit our growth.

MEMORY

DEPENDING ON WHAT IT IS THAT WE HAVE TO REMEMBER, WE HAVE TO DIG MORE OR LESS DEEP INTO OUR MEMORY, TO GET TO KNOW WHERE WE ARE. SOME OF US MAY SOMETIMES DIG AS DEEP DOWN AS OUR CHILDHOOD, WHILE SOME OF US WILL HAVE TO DIG DEEPER INTO OUR PAST LIFE OR LIVES.

NO MATTER IF IT IS AN EATING HABIT, SPIRITUAL QUESTION, A RELATIONSHIP OR A BUSINESS OPPORTUNITY, WE HAVE TO KNOW WHERE WE ARE, AND WE HAVE TO BE AS HONEST AS WE POSSIBLY CAN BE TO OURSELVES.

REASON

WHEN WE HAVE GONE BACK TO SEE WHERE WE ARE, NO MATTER IF IT IS A WEEK AGO, OR TO OUR CHILDHOOD, OR FORMER LIFE/LIVES, WE HAVE TO KNOW WHERE WE ARE AND WHERE WE ARE GOING. BEFORE WE CREATED IT IN OUR DREAMS, IMAGINATION OR IN A MORE INTUITIVE WAY, AND NOW WE REASON ABOUT IT AND THINK IN A MORE CONCRETE, DENSE WAY.

THEN THE REASONING WILL FOCUS ON EVERY OPPORTUNITY WE GET TO IMPROVE OUR RELATIONSHIP SO THAT IT CAN BECOME AN IDEAL RELATIONSHIP. IT IS A CONSCIOUS CHOICE WHERE WE HAVE TO BE ALIVE AND THINKING IN EVERY SITUATION THAT WE EXPERIENCE. ASK: WHAT CAN I IMPROVE IN THIS SITUATION? AND THEN CREATE SITUATIONS THAT ARE IMPROVING SUBSEQUENTLY.

3, THINKING-REASONING

We have special focus on building up our self-image and our common self-image in the Love-Relationship. When we have consciously been evaluating ourselves and tried to see where we are compared to where we are going, our goal, it's time to think and see ourselves in different situations with our new goal, our ideal Love-Relationship and our spouse.

Not only as we did in the past exercises when we were seeing ourselves together with our Love-Mate in pictures and movies.

We should think and act as if it already has happened that we have become that person together with our spouse that we want to become.

Now I don't mean that we shall do something that may hurt or compete with somebody else in a conscious negative way, we have to think (and act) with respect both to ourselves and others.

Actually this is a time for building up our self-esteem, self-image and our winning image of ourselves, and if we already are in a relationship and working with our spouse we can do it together.

> Ask: Do we have a loving winning image alone and/or together?
>
> And what are the common factors?

We may not know how we will get to our ideal Love-relationship. That is why we just have to believe and have faith and have a strong self-image.

Have you ever thought about that you together with your spouse can have an image that is loving, romantic, winning, radiant, etc?

And if you are alone you can still work with your own self-image so it becomes loving, romantic, winning, radiant etc and imagine yourself with your future spouse in your ideal Love-Relationship.

First see your spouse and yourself together and ask yourself:

> What do we/I look like?
> How are/am we/I dressed?
> What do we/I radiate.
> How do we behave towards each other, ourselves and others?
> What morality do we/I have?
> How often do we/I say I love you, and with a genuine meaning?
> Do we like to touch each other?
> Do we like to touch each other in front of others?
> How can we behave towards each other when we are among other people?
> Can I be myself with my beloved spouse?
> Do I allow my spouse to be himself/herself?

When we think and work with our common and our own future image we can see where we are compared to where we want to be with our spouse and with ourselves.

3, THINKING, REASONING, MEMORY

This exercise opens up for us to see and reason how we want to behave and act and afterwards compare where we are with the help of our memory.

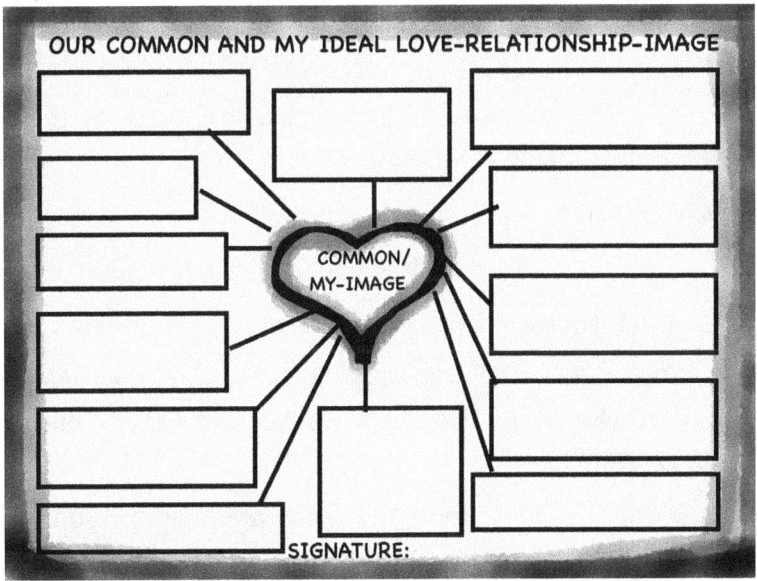

We use our higher faculties, REASON and MEMORY, to explore and develop.

It's a true science to bring forth our innermost desires of how we love to treat our spouse, ourselves and how we want to be treated, and also what we want to tell the world around us by our common and own behaviour, radiance and appearance.

> Are we in agreement with our spouse if we are in an Ideal Love-Relationship?
>
> Do we see ourself already experiencing our ideal Love-Relationship?

There are many things to think about...

There is another way to find out if our present ideal Love-Relationship is indeed ideal.

Ask yourself:

    Do I like to be in the company of my spouse?

    Do I thrive with him/her?

The Magic (law) Of Vibration is an underlying Magic (law) Of The Magic (law) Of Cause And Effect and it clearly states:

If we don't go well together with another person we don't vibrate on the same frequency, if one of us is more positive than the other and one is more negative than the other. We can also have different good or bad karmas (exchanges of giving and receiving) from the past with different people and that has an effect on the relationships we have today.

So you never have to feel guilty about anything, just learn from what you can see and experience and make the best of the situation where you are.

Then create in your mind how you want to experience situations differently and how to improve them in the future instead.

"WHEN YOU CHANGE OR IMPROVE AS A PERSON, YOUR ENVIRONMENT AND SURROUNDINGS CHANGE TO REFLECT THIS IMPROVEMENT."

BOB PROCTOR

"THE PERFECT IDEA IS THE IDEA YOU'RE EMOTIONALLY INVOLVED WITH."

BOB PROCTOR

 # CHAPTER 7

THE IDEAL LOVE-RELATIONSHIP AND THE SEVEN MAGIC GOAL STEPS TO SUCCESS! 4, IN LOVE

1. THE INSTANT INFATUATION (PASSION)

KEYWORDS: PERCEPTION, OBSERVATION AND EMOTIONS.

The higher faculty of the mind we use here is perception ... AND that is in the beginning when we are up flying high!!!

That is when the heart is emotionally involved and we through feelings vibrate and develop a new Love-Relationship and a new FREEDOM/paradigm(when consciously chosen).

Falling IN LOVE is like being the bud stretching towards the sun on it's way to full bloom and so we stretch towards our beloved Love-Mate with our increasing love ... thirsting for more love ... When the emotional part of our approach to our ideal Love-Relationship starts we can in the beginning only watch ourselves and our spouse/Love-Mate falling more and more in love with each other. our goal! We are in an observation state where we observe our feelings with our perception in the first of the following three steps which are the three necessary steps of falling in love for the Ideal Successful Love-Relationship.

Three necessary ways of falling IN LOVE for a successful Love-Relationship.

1. The instant infatuation (passion)
2. The developing infatuation (passion)
3. The playful infatuation (passion)

In this first stage of **IN LOVE** we start with number one:

1. THE INSTANT INFATUATION (PASSION)

This happens often and sometimes instantly when you meet your Ideal Spouse. You can also get that feeling within in your own body, but the actual big click is when you get the instant infatuation and become passionately IN LOVE with your spouse or future spouse. It hits you strongly and you are almost unable to think clearly when **The Instant Infatuation** develops within your body. You may be so totally IN LOVE that you don't know what to do with yourself. (helplessly IN LOVE)

If you are one of those who met your Ideal future spouse and fell IN LOVE instantly and you both agreed to build and share your Ideal Love-Relationship life together I want to congratulate you!

If you are one of those who met your Ideal future spouse, but you for some reason could not get together and share a common life despite the fact you fell IN LOVE with him/her or both of you fell IN LOVE with each other then you have to learn to master yourself and take one or several steps backwards and analyze the situation. Everything in this world depends on 'Universal Magics' (laws) and there is also a 'Science Of The Soul'.

Chapter 7

The universal magic (law) 'The Magic (law) Of Cause And Effect' (exchanges of giving and receiving) is a major Magic (law) that governs most actions we do.

When we meet a potential Ideal Love-Spouse/Love-Mate things don't always go as we would like because of that Magic (law), but when it works we can allow ourselves to be head over heals IN LOVE. Fill in what you or both of you experience and how you experience it.

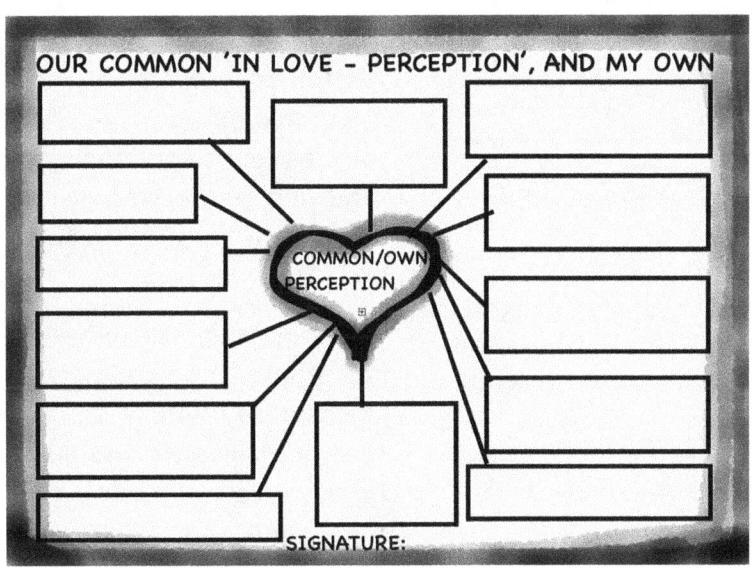

4, IN LOVE

WE OBSERVE WITH OUR PERCEPTION WHAT WE EXPERIENCE BEING IN LOVE.

When the heart is emotionally involved, and we through feelings vibrate and develop a new Love-Relationship.

We fall IN LOVE and it vibrates into our subconscious, emotional mind and we become emotionally involved in the Love-Relationship.

1 The instant infatuation has started and we begin, like the bud which is reaching towards the sun for it's love, to stretch more LOVE.

The body is shaking when the new vibrations enter it from the mind and we experience an euphoric feeling of happiness.

4.IN LOVE

WHEN THE HEART IS EMOTIONALLY INVOLVED, AND WE THROUGH FEELINGS VIBRATE AND DEVELOP A NEW PARADIGM.

KEY WORDS:
PERCEPTION
OBSERVATION
EMOTIONS

"BUILD THE IMAGE AND KNOW IN YOUR HEART THE IMAGE WILL MATERIALIZE."

BOB PROCTOR

"THE GREATEST ASSET FOR <u>SUCCESSFUL COMMUNICATION</u> WOULD HAVE TO BE ONE'S ABILITY TO <u>LISTEN</u>."

BOB PROCTOR

 # CHAPTER 8

FEAR => COMMUNICATION => KNOWLEDGE
THE SEVEN MAGIC GOAL STEPS TO SUCCESS, 5. GRATITUDE AND FORGIVENESS

To overcome fear necessitates good communication. Communication is the basic foundation for a successful relationship.

In order to be in a constant gratitude and forgiveness state we have to prepare ourselves and overcome fear.

2. THE DEVELOPING INFATUATION (PASSION)

This is very essential to work with for those who want a VERY SUCCESSFUL IDEAL LOVE-RELATIONSHIP!

Face the fear and fear will leave you, be brave.

Most people have paradigms (multitude of habits) that after a while in 1, THE INSTANT INFATUATION state will try to take over the new and loving feelings that we experience with the result that most people stop being IN LOVE or love weakens and fades away.

If we want to stay in THE IN LOVE state, both partners have to consciously be involved with the process and actively work together so that they overcome all the fear that may pop up.

This can stretch over a longer period of time where both Love-Partners (spouses) have to want to consciously participate in the developing work in The Love-Relationship.

When we meet fear and obstacles, it is very essential that we are open for each other and show our weaker sides to each other. COMPASSION and LOVE are very important.

Ask yourself and your Spouse, Love-Mate: What scares me and us? What do we need to talk about to release tensions between us?

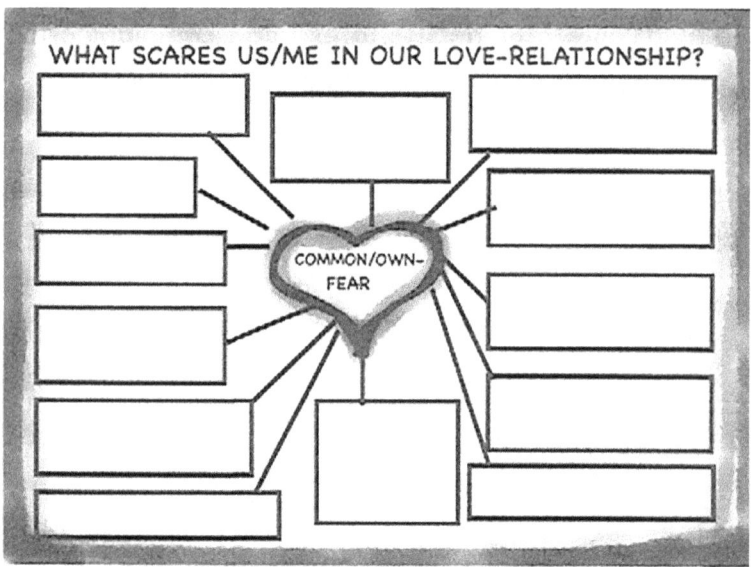

We learn to become more communicative when we open up to our spouse, and we can also develop these qualities alone so that we can be more ready for our Ideal Love-Relationship when it enters into our lives. When we are honest with ourselves and our Spouse and/or Love-Mate we develop a strength that can lead to the immeasurably beautiful life we can develop together. It's a constant communication we have internally with ourselves, and if possible even with our spouse, Love-Mate and externally with our Spouse, Love-Mate.

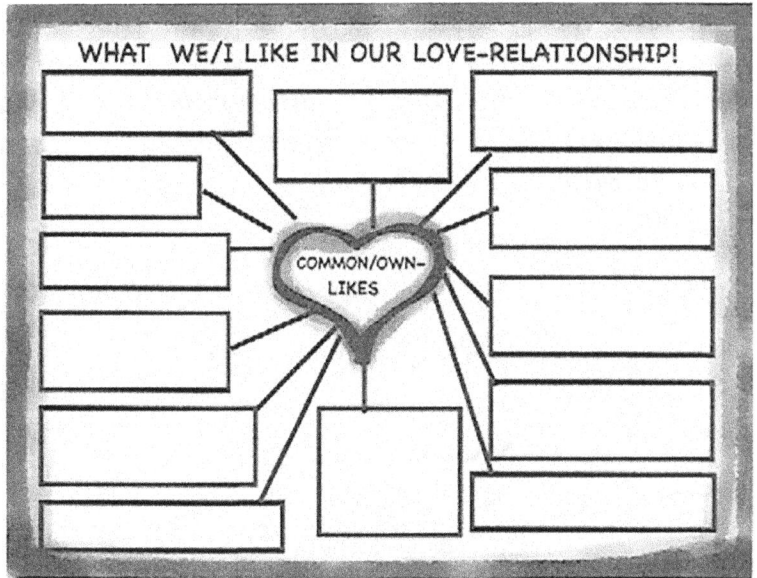

When you face fear go to the opposite and think of how you would like to be instead. Then make a heart of what you like and want that is positive.

2, THE DEVELOPING INFATUATION (PASSION)

This is where we examine each other and ourselves and fall more and more IN LOVE with each other. The state is deeper rooted in the body and we are not yet 100% knowing each other or ourselves. This stage is a 'GETTING TO KNOW EACH OTHER' phase. We can even be a little insecure with each before we know how the other person is working, thinking and acting in general.

Along the way we use our 'Higher Faculties Of The Mind': PERCEPTION and REASON. We shall also be aware of the other persons perception as well as our own. We also use reasoning as we have to reason a lot to overcome our fears. Be each others 'BEST FRIENDS'!

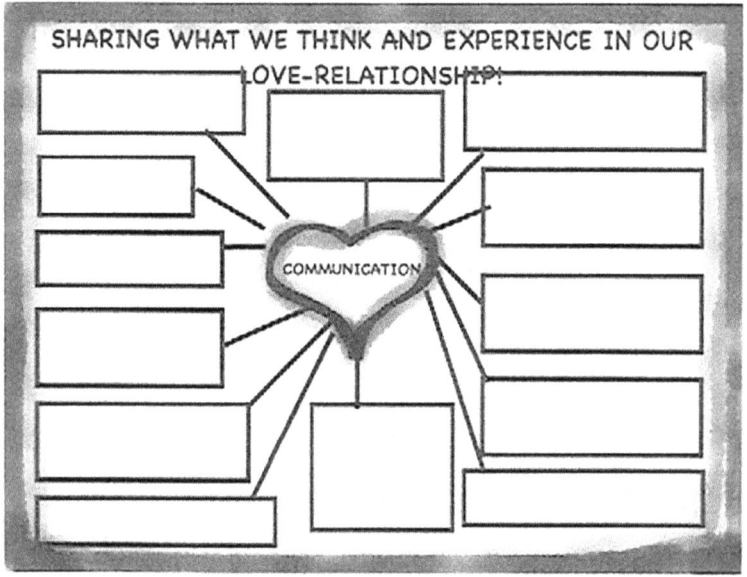

When we learn to share with each other and support each other and communicate with each other, we basically remove fear and replace it with trust. We learn to trust and respect each other. These exercises are the essential beginning of 5, Gratitude and Forgiveness in 'Seven Magic Goal Steps To Success'.

"FEAR AND FAITH BOTH DEMAND YOU TO BELIEVE IN SOMETHING YOU CANNOT SEE, YOU CHOOSE!"

BOB PROCTOR

"<u>PERSISTENCE</u> IS AS INTERWOVEN WITH SUCCESS AS THE CHICKEN IS WITH THE EGG."

BOB PROCTOR

CHAPTER 9

SOUL-MATES AND KARMA-MATES

(Karma=exchanges of giving and receiving) and the difference. The ultimate Love-Relationship with the least negative Karma-Clouds as possible.

PERSISTENCE AND PERSEVERANCE = LOVING PATIENCE TOWARDS OURSELVES AND OTHERS.

THE IDEAL LOVE-RELATIONSHIP AND THE SEVEN MAGIC GOAL STEPS TO SUCCESS 5, GRATITUDE AND FORGIVENESS.

We are still working with **2, THE DEVELOPING INFATUATION (PASSION)**

To be in a state of constant gratitude and forgiveness we have to work persistently and with perseverance and be very loving and patient towards ourselves and others.

When we have a goal to get to our Ideal Love-Relationship, it may seem that we are giving up at times, but if we are PERSISTENT and PERSEVERE we will always come back to the path again. And if the desire is strong enough we will always come back on track again. There are however a huge difference between Soul-Mates and only Karma-Mates. (karma=exchanges of giving and receiving)

Living and sharing our lives with our Soul-Mate is THE ULTIMATE IDEAL LOVE-RELATIONSHIP when there are the least karma-clouds possibly. In this relationship we are happier than ever. If we can combine it with our own spiritual development it's even better and gives us everlasting results when applied wisely.

So how do we verify and know who is our Soul-Mate and what is our Soul-Mate?

As I have a Soul-Master and I communicate telepathically with him and have also received some messages from him, I have his permission to share some of the messages with you:

Words to explain:

> Satsangis = People initiated by a <u>perfect living Soul-Master</u>
>
> Sach Khand = The highest spiritual Region
>
> Soul-Master = Perfect Living Soul-Master

"SOUL-MATES LOST IN WORLDLY GAMES

Soul-Mates are special for each other.

We only have one Soul-Mate. When we come into the universe as one Soul it gets divided into two parts and when it comes into the physical form you can still be born as two women or two men or one of each sex although we come into the universe as one female energy and one male energy and when we merge back to Sach Khand with the help of our Soul-Master we find our own energy that we had when we entered the universe which is either male or female.

When we are in the world we can be lost in the worldly game not knowing who our Soul-Mate is, and as a satsangi we open up to merge back to our own origin, and we open up to become consciously aware of our own Soul. Then we can recognize our own Soul-Mate if we get the grace to meet the Soul-Mate in this life.

And for ages and lifetimes we may not have been aware of our own Soul-Mate who in fact is the other half of our own Soul. We could have shared our lives with each other in countless lifetimes and most of the time the love we have for our Soul-Mate is enormous and somehow we feel that there is something special with the other person who is our Soul-Mate.

Often we have developed stronger and stronger love-bonds between each other in many lifetimes which become stronger the more spiritually aware we are. We understand that there has to be a give and receive between different people so although there may be instant LOVE between two Soul-Mates they may have to pay off more karma before they can get together and share their lives in the physical. Then it can seem like they are lost in the worldly game, but the more developed and aware they are, the more conscious they are about this.

And one day they will both merge back to their common Soul and get united there for always as they move together as one Soul to Sach Khand through their Soul-Master's grace.

The Soul-Master is guiding two initiated Soul-Mates who originated from one Soul in coordination so that they are close to each other in their development, and mostly have a chance to merge back together even as they live as humans on earth. That's THE ULTIMATE LOVE-RELATIONSHIP they both have a chance to experience when the karma are good and when they get a chance to develop their spiritual side by meditating 2 1/2 hours daily after the instructions of their Soul-Master that they received at the initiation day from the representative in the country or region where they live.

Then they can both become consciously aware of their own common Soul and get the most beautiful spiritual experiences together. That's the highest gift we can experience here on earth before we are ready for Sach Khand where we get shoulder to shoulder with our Soul-Master in awareness."

"COMING TOGETHER WITH SOUL-MATES AND HOW YOU CAN UPLIFT EACH OTHER.

Once we have identified our Soul-Mate at a deeper level we should think about how we can help each other the most and we should learn to identify which one of us is the stronger and which one of us needs the most help from the other Soul-Mate. When we know that, we can either make something bad or something good out of it. And as we have a goal to come to Sach Khand and go to the audible, positive, creative lifestream in order to get there, of course we want to be positive.

We work of course at first with ourselves and meditate 2 1/2 hours daily after the instructions of our Soul-master that we received at the initiation day from the representative in the country or region where we live. The more we know about ourselves and our inner life the more we can share with our Soul-Mate and the more we can help our Soul-Mate too. We should not share our inner spiritual experiences with each other unless we have come very, very far both of us. We can share all the mind experiences at

Chapter 9

first and make sure that we are at the same level with each other.

And then very carefully work with our inner life until both of us have conquered the mind.

Once the mind is conquered for both Soul-Mates they can meet on the inside and work together as one Soul all the way to Sach Khand with the help and guidance of the Soul-Master.

So when both Soul-Mates have conquered their minds they both know it at a deeper level and if they have good communication they will know exactly where the other person is and then they automatically go together on the inner planes to Sach Khand and it is so beautiful for the Soul-Master to see two Soul-Mates that go side by side to their common goal to Sach Khand. They are in tune and in harmony with each other at a very deep level and those Soul-Mates can go very far in their spiritual development, and also on the inside share it with each other.

That will not be a pain like we can experience it in the world when you can't share something on the outside, it will be true joy instead when you can share things on the inside and enjoy each others company on the inside as well.

When we trust our Soul-Master and have faith in the process that we need to go through, we will one day wake up to and see that all the fairytales about our Soul-Master and Soul-Mate actually were true, then we will be the happiest being ever and forever grateful to our Soul-Master who led us all the way to his home in Sach Khand that also turned out to be our home and that is all **LOVE.**"

SPIRITUAL LOVE-LIFE VS. WORLDLY LOVE-LIFE

"The Ideal Love-Life

Spiritual Love-life: Soul-Mate, Best Friend, Husband/Wife, Lover/Mistress

—Versus—

Worldly Love-Life: Lover/Mistress, Husband/Wife, Best Friend and Soul-Mate

When we study the Soul and the mind and learn that everything comes from within, then it's natural to build up a relationship at first from within, so that the love grows instead of vanishes.

And especially when we get a chance to meet our Soul-Mate when it is our last life here on earth we are connected forever, but we should start as Best Friends and build a steadfast ground for our relationship and support each other in everything we do, then the love grows and when we have come that far we can decide to get married and support each other as a family business. And the last step we can go to after that is to become Lover and Mistress. Then we are totally confident in the relationship and we can rely on each other and feel safe with each other.

A relationship that goes all the way from the Soul to the Lover/Mistress level is a relationship that lasts for a lifetime when you are willing to work with the relationship. There is the whole base of a successful Love-Life, where communication and understanding are the most important things to make a relationship work. This is The Spiritual Ideal Love-Life versus The Worldly Love-Life as follows:

Chapter 9

When we meet a person of the opposite sex, we make love at first because we feel the attraction; that can make us very puzzled since we don't know the person we are so intimate with. We have no idea where the relationship will go and develop since we cannot see what we will do with this person.

Do we have to make love or can we just do business with them? Attraction can be used in many ways and we have to figure out if we have to make love with everyone we meet that we are attracted to, or if we will have another relationship with them.

When we have made love with the person in the worldly life and the attraction is still there we often get married to each other and form a family.

We are still often insecure with each other as we are not consciously connected with each other from within. When the attraction is over we don't feel anything in general and then we say the love is over and many people get divorced.

But there are a few who manage to become Best Friends on their journey through life together. Many people say we are at least good friends and if they are Soul-Mates they have a chance to be really good friends, good husbands and wives and functioning lovers and mistress. And <u>VERY</u> seldom in the end they discover that they are Soul-Mates if they are.

Time can be unnecessarily wasted in being insecure in the beginning in a Worldly Love-Life when we don't take the time to get to know each other and only make love in the beginning. To figure out what the other person wants to do is very important before we build a relationship with somebody without building a Love-Relationship with marriage and family. Maybe we only have a shorter karma with a person, then we can do it in another way that is healthier and more creative in the long run.

Getting to know each other is the first step to success in a Love-Life. To get a Soul-Connection is more rare, as we only have one Soul-Mate, but that is the basics for Soul-Mates. Then build a solid grounding based on where we want to go in life, in a direction that is common for both. That is The Ideal Spiritual Love-Life that is the best in the long run and The Worldly Love-Life is rarely so successful.

We are more honest with each other in a Spiritual Love-Life where we communicate better with each other in general.

The Soul-Master supports and works with Soul-Mates, as it is the most harmonious Love-Relationship we can have. It's best for our Soul and our spiritual development.

So when we don't have karma with somebody else but our Soul-Mate the Soul-Master loves to put us together with our Soul-Mate.

If we are not together with our Soul-Mate we can always practice as if we were together with him or her, then we create good karma so that we have a chance to be happy in the end of our life-times with or without our Soul-Mate."

Chapter 9

DIFFERENT ROLES IN DIFFERENT LIFETIMES AS HUMANS. (HOMOSEXUALITY)

We play different roles in different lifetimes as humans. Sometimes we are born as a woman and sometimes as a man and it can vary from life to life, but often we have our favourite sex as we are coming into the universe with a little more of the feminine or masculine touch. We may prefer to be either a woman or a man. There are even those who don't feel at home at all being born as the opposite sex and some people even change sex because of that, and some people become homosexual because of that.

Therefore we should have an understanding of people who don't feel at home in their bodies when they prefer to be a man or a woman.

They should also know that in their next life they most likely will turn back to their favourite sex, so therefore there is nothing to worry about and sometimes our lives are not 100% ideal and according to our desires.

Soul-Mates and other Souls that are close to each other can even come into this world as the same sex in certain incarnations which explains why they can get attracted to each other in a relationship like for example a marriage, so people should have more understanding for those attractions and relationships.

Sometimes we have to pay karma in a different way too that is not ideal. Then we don't have to feel inferior to other people just because we have to go through a strange karma.

'The Magic (law) Of Cause And Effect' is the reigning Magic (law) in the universe, so we have to obey and adjust to the different exchanges of give and receive when we are supposed to do that."

This is a background for what we need to know about Soul-Mates and Karma-Mates enjoy it wisely!

"YOU HAVE BEEN GIFTED WITH MENTAL FACULTIES TO IMPROVE ANY CIRCUMSTANCES AROUND YOU."

BOB PROCTOR

"THE MORE <u>GRATEFUL</u> YOU ARE, THE CLOSER YOU BECOME TO THE SPIRITUAL CORE OF YOUR BEING."

BOB PROCTOR

CHAPTER 10

LOVE, SEX AND ROMANCE AND OTHER EMOTIONS

- <u>LEARN TO RECOGNIZE YOUR EMOTIONS</u>

- <u>GRATITUDE OPENS UP FOR THE HIGHEST FACULTY OF THE MIND-COMPASSION</u>

- <u>THE IDEAL LOVE-RELATIONSHIP AND THE SEVEN MAGIC GOAL STEPS TO SUCCESS!</u>

- <u>5, GRATITUDE AND FORGIVENESS</u>

    To overcome the seven negative emotions and replace them with the seven peaceful and neutral emotions and the seven positive emotions filled with compassion and love for the Lord, ourselves and others.

    KEY WORDS: COMPASSION, LOVE, HAPPINESS, BELIEF AND FAITH.

    <u>2, THE DEVELOPING INFATUATION (PASSION)</u>

To overcome the seven negative emotions and replace them with the seven neutral emotions and the seven positive emotions filled with COMPASSION and LOVE for ourselves, our spouse and others.

Everyone who wants a successful ideal Love-Relationship strives for happiness and harmony, and when we work with ourselves and are in tune with our spouse and Loved-One it is possible that we together can experience this happiness and harmony.

This is what THE DEVELOPING INFATUATION (PASSION) is all about, we get to know more about ourselves and the other person. If we learn to identify our feelings we can let go of the negative feelings and become grounded in middle, neutral, Peaceful, Shushumna channel where we are feeling very harmonious and peaceful, before we move upward with our positive feelings in the positive creative, productive, sound current, the Pingala stream on the right.

Feelings can affect us negatively, peacefully and positively.

Why do I tell you all this?

Because if we didn't know it before it's about time to know that we will benefit the whole body when we learn to heal our negative feelings and automatically become more and more grounded in the neutral, Peaceful lifestream and so the more negative baggage we can let go of.

Q: What is exactly happening when we let go of negative feelings?

Chapter 10

A: We pay off negative karma (exchanges of giving and receiving) and the more we pay the lighter our karmic load will become, but we just have to watch out that we don't create new karma that will keep us within the universal realms.

First of all, I will give you a chart about how you can more easily identify where you are and use the benefits shown in the chart where you are in your feelings.

First make a similar chart to what I have here. Learn to master it yourself before you do it together with your spouse/Love-Mate.

If we do this too early with our spouse/Love-Mate there is the risk that we will get into a blame-game where we see all the bad in the other person and see ourselves as much better than them!

Identify where you are right now and put one of the index stickers in one of the boxes in front of the words that matches you right now. Maybe you feel several things and then you just use several index stickers. Then remove them when you don't agree with the feelings any more.

If you find it difficult to identify your own feelings you can start out by identifying the feelings of the people that you have around you without pointing a finger at them and blaming them in a negative way. Just do it gently, you don't even need to speak with them about it. Learn to see where they are, then try it with yourself. Now we have learned more about how to identify the different emotions subsequently.

We may even have identified emotions that may be old karmas (exchanges of giving and receiving).

THE SUB CONSCIOUS AND EMOTIONAL MIND
LEARN TO IDENTIFY NEGATIVE, PEACEFUL AND POSITIVE KARMA

WHAT UPSETS YOU, WHAT MAKES YOU PEACEFUL AND WHAT MAKES YOU HAPPY?

THE SEVEN NEGATIVE EMOTIONS	THE SEVEN PEACEFUL EMOTIONS	THE SEVEN POSITIVE EMOTION
FEAR	PEACEFUL	LOVE
GREED	SERENE	ROMANCE
JEALOUSY	CALM	DESIRE
SUPERSTITION	HARMONIOUS	ENTHUSIASM
REVENGE	SATISFIED	HOPE
ANGER	COMFORTED	FAITH
HATRED	SECURE	SEX

THE MAGIC (LAW) OF CAUSE AND EFFECT, GIVING AND RECEIVING

Identify where you are right now and put one of the index stickers in one of those boxes next to the emotion that matches you right now. Maybe you feel several things and then you use several index stickers. Then remove them when you don't agree with the feelings.

Chapter 10

Now we have come to the next step: FORGIVENESS How do we learn to forgive?

There are certainly several ways to forgive, but I have found that THE EXERCISES OF THE HEART are very efficient!

As long as we need the heart diagrams we shall keep them to help us release all the old emotions and move in the direction of our goal.

Now make a heart of FORGIVENESS! COMPASSION is The highest 'Faculty Of The Mind'.

Use the text of Forgiveness and forgive whoever and whatever it was that made me/us so upset.

Use this whenever you are in your feelings and have difficulty letting go of an emotion that disturbs you.

Remember if we learn to LET GO of emotions that disturb us, we learn to pay off the karmas faster and we don't hold onto something that doesn't benefit us.

As soon as we indulged in too many negative feelings we can be sure that there are karmas involved. (exchanges of giving and receiving) COMPASSION is the highest 'FACULTY OF THE MIND' that we are working with, and when we 'let go and let God' we let the higher awareness, that we call God or whatever we choose to call it, take over when we have done our best.

Then we release a lot by doing so, and afterwards we become filled with GRATITUDE when we have been able to let go of old paradigms (multitude of habits) and old karmas (stored exchanges of giving and receiving).

COMPASSIONATE, EMOTIONAL FORGIVENESS

When we experience an emotion that is in the way for our HAPPINESS we choose to release the emotion by first identifying it and then FORGIVING IT.

Then we say three times (and write if we want): I forgive WHOEVER (if we know) Name _____ (it can also be ourself) who has caused me to feel this way _____ so that it affected me to feel this way _____ despite it isn't true.

I forgive myself for having reacted this way _____.
I am now free to move on with a peaceful mind.

This a very good exercise to let go of resentment which is a mixture of disappointment, anger and fear. Let LOVE find it's way back to your heart by learning to forgive both yourself, your ongoing Love-Relationship and others both for what you or he/she or others said or did/do to upset you.

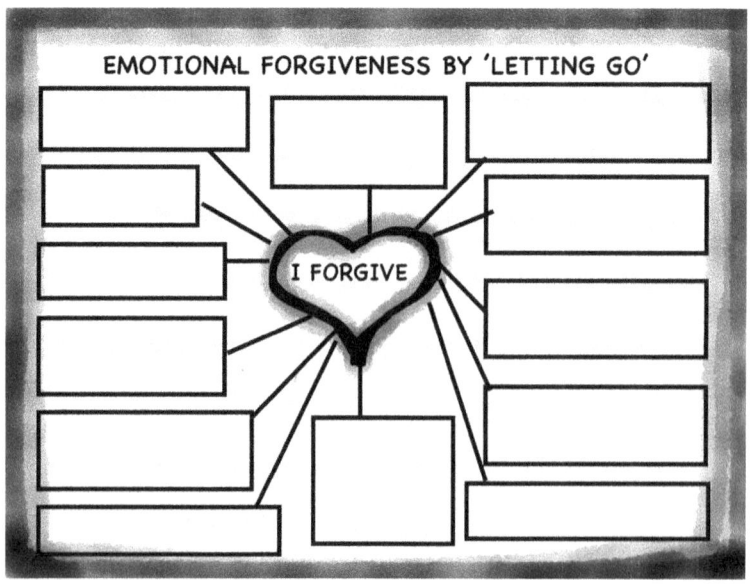

Chapter 10

GRATEFUL FOR EMOTIONS BOTH POSITIVE, PEACEFUL AND NEGATIVE

Fill in the EMOTIONS that benefit you and that you are grateful for both positive, peaceful and negative, (sometimes negative feelings can make you grow) about your present FEELINGS and if you need more hearts make them! Now we have sorted out what was heavy for us and what was easy for us. In general we don't have a problem with what we liked or like, but we can become more inspired by our own good FEELINGS so that we can create our ideal Love-Relationship more easily. To be inspired of all the good that we already have experienced is a good reminder when we are feeling down knowing that we actually have experienced something good too.

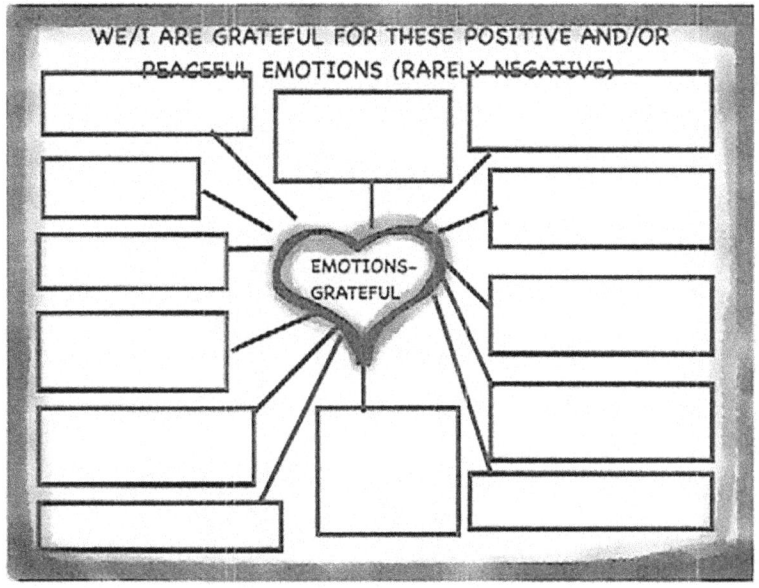

This exercise can help you to appreciate yourself, and if you have one, your present Love-Relationship and maybe turn it into an ideal Love-Relationship.

By going through these exercises every time you need to, you are actually working with your own 2, THE DEVELOPING INFATUATION, both with yourself and/or if you have and want to do it with your spouse/Love-Mate.

The more we learn to forgive and to be grateful for and the more we open our hearts with COMPASSION for each other and ourselves, the HAPPIER we become.

When we go through this process it is also important to believe in the good and trust the process as we develop our LOVE and COMPASSION for ourselves and others.

Chapter 10

5. GRATITUDE AND FORGIVENESS
GRATITUDE IS WHEN WE LET GO AND LET HARMONY TAKE PLACE IN OUR HEART. WE "LET GO AND LET GOD", WE LET GO OF CONTROL AND FEAR AND NEGATIVE FEELINGS AND WE FORGIVE OTHERS AND OURSELVES. WE DEVELOP COM-PASSION FOR OUR-SELVES AND OTHERS.

KEY WORDS:
COMPASSION
LOVE
HAPPINESS
BELIEVE
FAITH

-5, GRATITUDE AND FORGIVENESS

WE LEARN COMPASSION AS THE HIGHEST FACULTY OF THE MIND AND WE COME IN DEEPER CONTACT WITH OUR FEELING AND LEARN TO RECOGNIZE DEEPER EMOTIONS THAT CAN SIT AS BLOCKS IN OUR SYSTEM AND WHEN THEY ARE RELEASED WE CAN LET GO OF THEM.

WE ALSO PAY OFF KARMAS BY PAYING WITH OUR EMOTIONS, WITH THE HELP OF 'THE MAGIC (LAW) OF CAUSE AND EFFECT', EVEN CALLED 'THE MAGIC (LAW) OF KARMA (EXCHANGES RECEIVING) WHEN A KARMA IS PAID MAGIC HAPPENS!

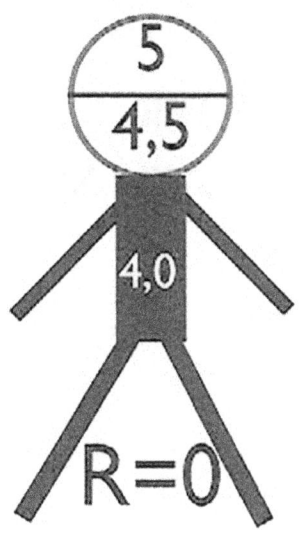

"GRATITUDE IS AN ATTITUDE THAT HOOKS US UP TO THE SOURCE OF SUPPLY. AND THE MORE GRATEFUL YOU ARE, THE CLOSER YOU BECOME TO YOUR MAKER, TO THE ARCHITECT OF THE UNIVERSE, TO THE SPIRITUAL CORE OF YOUR BEING. IT'S A PHENOMENAL LESSON."

BOB PROCTOR

"YOU CAN CHOOSE TO DEVELOP YOUR <u>WILL</u> AND STAY FOCUSED ON YOUR CHOSEN OBJECTIVE UNTIL YOU GET THE <u>RESULTS</u> YOU WANT."

BOB PROCTOR

 # CHAPTER 11

YOU GET TO YOUR RESULTS BY MOVING WITH ACTIONS OF LOVE AND A JOYFUL, PLAYFUL ATTITUDE

THE IDEAL LOVE-RELATIONSHIP AND THE SEVEN MAGIC GOAL STEPS TO SUCCESS! 6 ACTIONS

Use your willpower and strength to move with actions into your new Love-Relationship.

3. THE PLAYFUL INFATUATION (PASSION)

KEY WORDS: WILLPOWER, STRENGTH, PLAYFULNESS

We move with love through the terror barrier into our new life with actions of LOVE. Actions give results. Now our goal is manifesting, our Ideal Love-Relationship that we have been working so hard for is manifesting. We are moving into our new freedom, our new comfort zone, with willpower and strength as we have released all the old heavy stuff we have been carrying around for so long.

3, THE PLAYFUL INFATUATION (PASSION)

This is the playful infatuation, where we have released so much old karma, paradigms (multitude of habits), tension and excess baggage that we now can allow ourselves to participate in the playful infatuation.

If we are single we can play ourselves, if we are a single and initiated by a perfect living Soul-Master we can play with him in our mind, and if we are so fortunate that we already are in a relationship, then we can continue to create our Ideal Love-Relationship and make it come true.

6. ACTIONS
MOVE WITH LOVE THROUGH THE TERROR BARRIER INTO YOUR NEW LIFE, WITH ACTIONS. ACTIONS GIVE RESULTS!

THE IDEAL LOVE-RELATIONSHIP AND THE SEVEN MAGIC GOAL STEPS TO SUCCESS!

KEY WORDS:
WILLPOWER STRENGTH

ADJUSTMENTS, CHANGE

6
5,6

6,7

R=6,7

YOU MOVE THROUGH THE TERROR BARRIOR WITH ACTIONS OF LOVE WHEN YOU ALLOW LOVE TO BE MORE POWERFUL THAN FEAR.

Chapter 11

Ideas and thoughts, that we were only playing with in our imagination, begin to take form in our real physical world. Love-Mates and Spouses can show up any time if we haven't seen or met them before. We can speak and act with them in a very playful, relaxed, happy and loving way.

To get to our final state, our final goal we may have to take action.

WE WANT TO LIVE IN OUR IDEAL LOVE-RELATIONSHIP!

Those actions often come to us subsequently but we can however make a plan and try to make it happen, but we should be very ready to change if we find it more important to do something else.

We can however make a heart where we write different action steps and still keep an open mind for changes. We must be very flexible too in order to reach our Ideal Love-Relationship. Things can change very fast ...

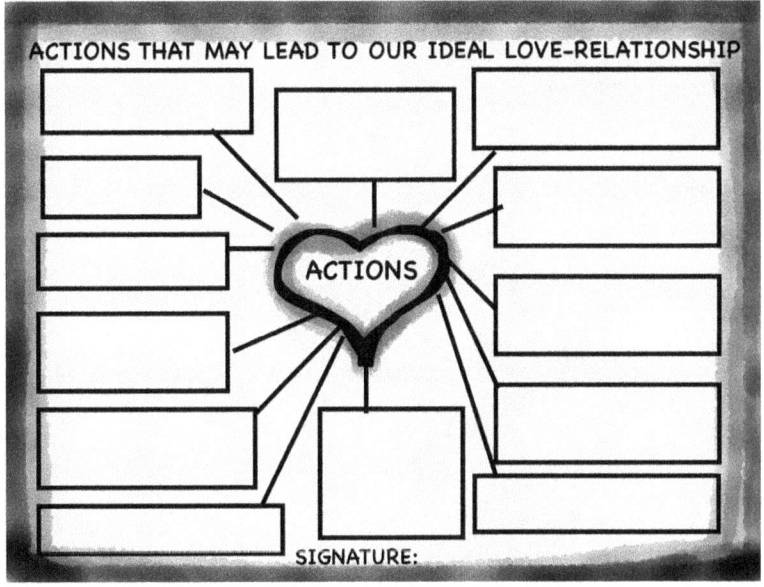

But during the other steps to success we have learned that we must persistently persevere and in this Magic Goal Step Of Action it's easier to allow ourselves to be in the playful infatuation (passion), where with words, gestures, actions in all kinds of ways we are playful and happy.

Things loosen up and we are more harmonious and happy and we still we use our willpower and strength to move ahead towards our new freedom that is opening up.

"LIFE CAN BE ABSOLUTELY PHENOMENAL, AND IT SHOULD BE! IT'S A MAGNIFICENT TRIP."

BOB PROCTOR

"NO AMOUNT OF READING OR MEMORIZING WILL MAKE YOU SUCCESSFUL IN LIFE. IT'S THE <u>UNDERSTANDING</u> AND <u>APPLICATION</u> OF WISE THOUGHT WHICH COUNTS."

BOB PROCTOR

 **CHAPTER 12**

WHAT IS A LIVING MIND-MASTER AND A PERFECT LIVING SOUL-MASTER

In order to keep and develop that beautiful ideal Love-Relationship it's necessary to study the teachings of both a living Mind-Master and a perfect living Soul-Master.

A living Mind-Master is someone who knows about how the universal Magics (laws) work in the Universe.

A Mind-Master masters also the universal realms and the human mind.

A Mind-Master that has not developed his/her inner spiritual knowledge with the help of a perfect living Soul-Master cannot go beyond the second inner spiritual region and the Mind-Master will not come out of 'the Wheel of 84' (8,400 000 species in the world). Unless the Mind-Master takes refuge in a perfect living Soul-Master, the Mind-Master will stay within the universal realms and most certainly be reborn as a human again, but there is no guarantee that the Mind-Master will remember all the good that the Mind-Master has learned as a Mind-Master in his/her next life, for that depends on the Mind-Master's karma.

The Mind-Master can teach people all about how to live in harmony with the universal Magics (laws) in the easiest way.

A Mind-Master reads people's minds and tries to do good for them under their present circumstances and can teach them how to improve their lives. But

Mind-Masters themselves can be so enchanted by the worlds admiration, which gives them everything they need, that they forget their own spiritual development, that would take them out of the universal realms, because they enjoy their worldly but short-lived gifts too much.

And even though the world seemingly may be lying at their feet, they ought to know that life here in this world is like a fleeting moment and everything can be taken away again in no time and that our purpose in life is not only to enjoy but to develop ourselves and be liberated and go back to our true origin and home.

There are however Mind-Masters who haven't learned to use their kindness and they can be a little tough compared to a perfect living Soul-Master who has developed his/her LOVE and COMPASSION for humanity and all living beings.

A perfect living Soul-Master holds the key to people's freedom outside of the universal realms.

Under his protection and guidance he/she liberates us from being born again and again and helps us pay off our karma in the easiest way so that we can be reunited with our Soul consciously and gain the same awareness as our perfect living Soul-Master.

"A GOAL GIVES YOU DIRECTION. YOU ARE ON A MISSION. YOU ARE ALIVE."

BOB PROCTOR

"IF YOU CAN SEE IT IN YOUR MIND, YOU CAN HOLD IT IN YOUR HAND."

BOB PROCTOR

 CHAPTER 13

YOUR DREAMS COME TRUE!!!

THE IDEAL LOVE-RELATIONSHIP AND THE SEVEN MAGIC GOAL STEPS TO SUCCESS! 7, THE GOAL, THE NEW FREEDOM - 3, THE PLAYFUL INFATUATION (PASSION)

Here we are ready to live 'The Fairytale' with-our Soul-Mate or Love-Mate.

It can be something like: I love you unconditionally!!! I accept and love you the way you are. ... The ultimate freedom!!!

Try to fulfil both your own and your Love-partner's dreams and sometimes it may be that we are in loving disagreements. We all have different ideals since we all have different desires to experience different things.

Since we have worked together or with ourselves through 'The Developing Infatuation' where we grow a lot in awareness through the developing education, when we have reached our NEW FREEDOM, our GOAL.

Then it becomes 'THE PLAYFUL INFATUATION', (PASSION), where we play with words, gestures, activities, and in different ways with each other and different things in life and it becomes fun because we have conquered the lower parts of ourselves and gained more awareness and maybe more success in the world as well as in our IDEAL LOVE-RELATIONSHIP.

CONGRATULATIONS! YOU MADE IT!

WHERE YOU WANT TO GO!

7. THE GOAL

RESULTS, NEW FREEDOM, NEW COMFORT ZONE. AWARENESS AND/OR EXPANSION.

KEY WORDS:
FREEDOM
AWARENESS
EXPANSION

"THE IDEAL LOVE-RELATIONSHIP"

THE IDEAL LOVE-RELATIONSHIP AND THE SEVEN MAGIC GOAL STEPS TO SUCCESS!

- 7, THE GOAL
- NEW FREEDOM THOUGHTS
- NEW FREEDOM EMOTIONS
- NEW FREEDOM VIBRATIONS
- NEW FREEDOM RESULTS
- THE NEW PARADIGM AND THE NEW IDEA HAS SUCCEEDED!

Chapter 13

HERE I SHARE WITH YOU PARTS OF WHAT I HAVE WRITTEN AS MY GOAL IN MY IDEAL LOVERELATIONSHIP:

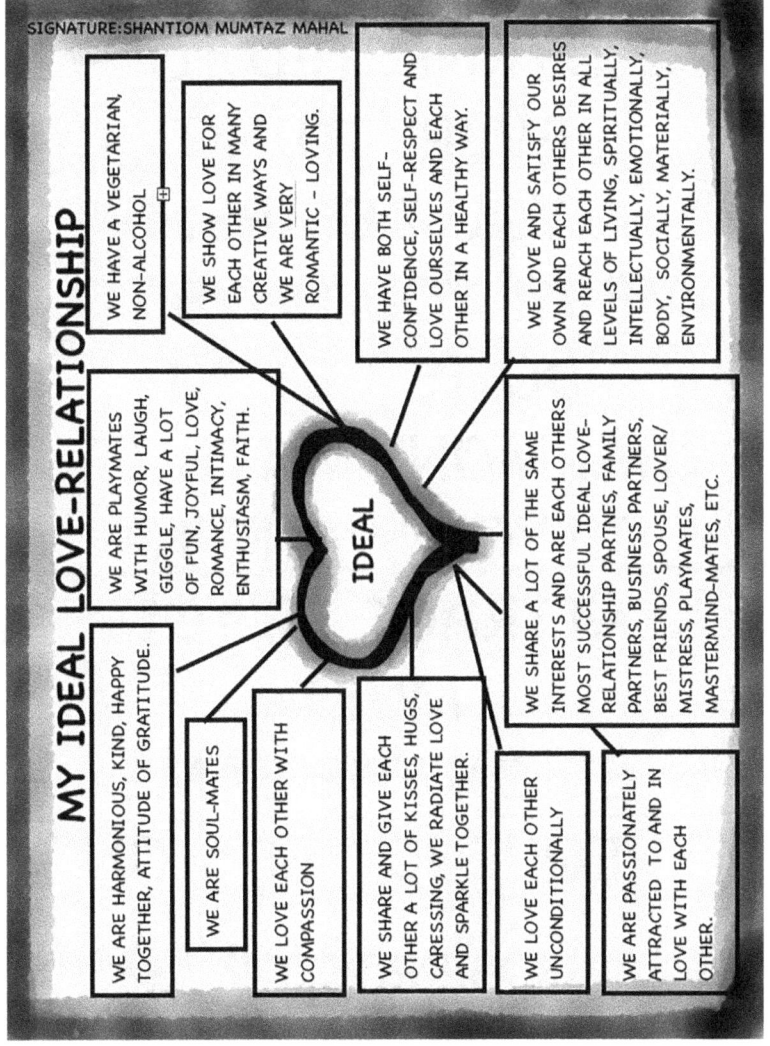

"YOU ARE ALREADY CONNECTED TO EVERYTHING YOU DESIRE. WHAT YOU HAVE TO DO IS GET IN HARMONY WITH IT. IF YOU WANT TO ATTRACT IT, YOU <u>MUST</u> BE ON THE SAME FREQUENCY IT'S ON."

BOB PROCTOR

"YOU HAVE BEEN GIFTED WITH MENTAL FACULTIES TO IMPROVE ANY CIRCUMSTANCE AROUND YOU."

BOB PROCTOR

 # CHAPTER 14

SUMMARY OF 'THE SEVEN MAGIC GOAL STEPS TO SUCCESS'

CONSTANTLY IMPROVING THE IDEAL LOVE-RELATIONSHIP TO KEEP IT SUCCESSFUL

This is a constant ongoing process that works with everything we do. The more consciously we think about the process the more consciously aware we are about what we shall do and what we are doing.

There are things that we are used to do we do automatically without thinking about the process although we go through it, but when we do things we haven't done before or that are important for us, we will be more aware of the process.

In 'THE SEVEN MAGIC GOAL STEPS TO SUCCESS' we use our 'SEVEN HIGHER FACULTIES OF THE MIND' to develop through 'THE SEVEN GOAL STEPS TO SUCCESS' to our goal.

Our 'SEVEN HIGHER FACULTIES OF THE MIND' are: INTUITION, IMAGINATION, MEMORY, REASON, PERCEPTION, COMPASSION AND WILL.

By using 'THE SEVEN HIGHER FACULTIES OF THE MIND' we develop our ability to use our conscious thinking and create something that can go far beyond our imagination as we use all the faculties of the mind.

Remember, once you have reached your IDEAL LOVE-RELATIONSHIP you should never stop Master

Minding about/with your spouse/Love-Mate to improve the Love-Relationship all the time, so that you can keep and develop the beautiful Love-Relationship that you once created to improve and let it grow to new dimensions all the time.

It is an ongoing process where you constantly try to take your relationship to a higher level and development.

Happier, more loving and more romantic among other things.

You should always strive for taking your Love-Relationship to a higher level!

WHAT IS YOUR VISION?

What is your vision about YOUR IDEAL LOVE-RELATIONSHIP?

MY VISION—LOVE CASTLE—LOVE COUPLES

My vision is to create a Love-Castle together with my Soul-Mate, where we can help Love-Couples to heal and get their relationship into full bloom.

"A GOAL GIVES DIRECTION... YOU ARE ON A MISSION. YOU ARE ALIVE."

BOB PROCTOR

SHANTIOM MUMTAZ MAHAL

Shantiom Mumtaz Mahal was born and live in Sweden. As she was the only child and her parents had several supermarkets she automatically started to work in her parents stores at a very young age and has continued it ever since.

But on the side she has educated herself and was quite active in the politics in her local and regional area and even at a young age she could see results of her actions in the society. Major things like free media and free choice of school for children were accepted by the parliament and government.

All her life she has been surrounded by animals, at first dogs and cats and when she had her own home and family all the extra animals where added like rabbits, horses, a parrot, fish, more cats and more dogs, which has really been an education in itself.

It has also been a fantastic experience for her to be a part of her family and experience the children's growth and her own, where karate has been an important common hobby for the whole family. Ballet and instruments have also played an important role in their lives.

From her early childhood her mother and grandmother have shared their great knowledge and love for gardening with her which she also has used a lot during her life.

Later on she has been educated in Polarity Therapy, Iridology, and Esoteric Science.

For many years Shantiom has been following the teachings of a perfect living Soul-Master which has greatly enriched her life.

In 2005 she started attending seminars with Bob Proctor, since then she has been educated as a LifeSuccess Consultant and attended several seminars and Matrixxs's. And she continues to study his teachings and now she is ready for the book business and sharing her knowledge with other people.

www.ingramcontent.com/pod-product-compliance
Lightning Source LLC
Chambersburg PA
CBHW070756100426
42742CB00012B/2157